What people are saying about
Starting! and Andrew Priestley

So many business advice books are written in a style that alienates and patronises the reader, who is often simply after guidance, clarity and knowledge. And business books can also be unnecessarily long and repetitive. Not Andrew's. Not this book. This is one of the best of this genre that I have read.

Starting! is written in an easy to understand format that is down to earth and easy to put in to practice.

Andrew's coaching skills and his own experience in business (warts and all) permeate the book, which makes this book very 'real' and easy to relate to.

The steps are easily applied by anyone serious about their business, and are communicated in a 'let's cut to the chase and get this done' way! For prospective business owners and those already running a business, this direct approach is invaluable.

A really useful book that I will re-read and refer to frequently.

Neil D'Silva, *Global Nutrition, The Gut Guru*

I can't believe the value within this book for the price. You are buying years of experience from a respected business coach. Like many other people I have business ideas, but putting them into practice seems overwhelming. Andrew takes his readers through the fundamentals of starting a business, because without these steps you risk losing a shed-load of money and time and will probably end up hating the business you once loved!

Andrew points out that our passion alone is highly unlikely to give us the lifestyle or fortune we crave, no matter how well meaning we are! The book has a simple format, but don't be fooled - you actually have to do the work! I am working through the ten questions and can already see that I need a viable business and not a hobby!

Nick Crossers, *Crossers Ltd* (UK)

In a strategy session, Andrew has an ability to 'unpack' your head in a relaxed and deliberate manner.

I was panicking and just couldn't get clarity. I was completely over thinking and looking too hard at the details, with a 'build it and they will come mentality'. Unachievable. Not now. The value I received from this process and *Starting!* has given me renewed motivation, direction and clarity. Implementation will follow. I am so grateful.

Melinda Mackay, *Sugar Free Solution (Australia)*

It is now several years since I first involved Andrew in my business and I am happy to say that since my business has thrived since then. I had been in business for over 20 years and as the business grew, I knew I was struggling to handle the many aspects of small business that mean the difference between success and failure. If you have a passion for what you do and the courage to make it happen, then I believe Andrew can help you get there.

John W Maslen, Managing Director, *ART Refrigeration* (Australia)

One of the best paradigms shifts I have ever had. From that one major shift, my business grew. Our turnover increased 90%. If I hadn't followed his advice, I'd still be a 'one man band'. The business has been a profitable concern since.

David Bentley, *Coastal Business Brokers (Australia)*

Andrew assisted the sales team and the operational team by giving us common threads by which to focus. The quantifiable results were a 25% increase in profit for our business and a substantial increase in our return business ensuring that the future will remain buoyant. We were coached in a way that genuinely enabled us to improve. Frustrating day-to-day challenges were solved effectively with clear thinking enabling more time to be focused on the business and growth.

Paul Stevens, GM, *Novotel Twin Waters* (Australia)

Andrew is one of the few coaches who genuinely walks his talk, and can deliver extraordinary results - fast. You want to learn from this guy. This guy can coach like no one I know and has an ability to kick things into overdrive! I'm living (and loving) the results daily. This process - captured in *Starting!* - is exceptional.

Doug Thomson, Manufacturer (UK)

I've done a million courses, read all the books and listened to all the tapes. In the context of all I've done to date. This strategy process stands alone as one of the best value, most enlightening personal and professional development experiences I have ever undertaken.

Paul Hourigan, *Retail Electronics* (Australia)

Do yourself a favour, and change the way you play your game. Andrew's coaching gives you the tools to reprogramme the functionality of the most valuable asset you control - *you!* It is the surest way I know to fast track your personal and professional success. This strategic approach was grounded and real and worth the effort that we applied to it as a team. Great value at five times the price.

Mark Tolley, *DTB Advertising* (Australia)

Andrew Priestley has developed a priceless gift that allows you to assess significance in a heartbeat and to skip past all the irrelevant details which have been clouding one's vision to hone in on the nugget that one had failed to see and in so doing to see past the problem to the solution in a way that feels like coming home. Sound too good to be true?

Well believe me it is true - I am continuing to work on my strategy and mission thanks to his intervention at a critical moment. Do not think twice about engaging in this approach with Andrew - he is a genius of understatement and will leave you inspired, encouraged and committed.

Dr Kim Joobst, *Functional Shift Consulting Ltd* (UK)

I attended a group strategy session. It was amazing. I learned a very impressive but easy to implement strategy for identifying the value in my business. Now I have a lot more clarity about developing my marketing strategy.

Anneta Pizag, *Pizag Ltd* (Australia)

In a fantastic strategy session, I learned more in 90 minutes than three decades of running businesses.

Tina Fotherby, *Famous Publicity* (UK)

I recently did a strategy session. I thought I had unpacked most of the value in my business but I was happily wrong to find out I was leaving a nice chunk on the table. If like me you think you have things figured out I highly recommend this approach to get fresh insights and stress test your ideas.

Chris Fyfe, Chris Fyfe Ltd (UK)

Starting!

**You might have a *good idea*
for a business but have you got
a *good business* for your idea?**

Andrew Priestley

WRITING MATTERS PUBLISHING

Starting!
Andrew Priestley
Copyright © 2017

Illustrations and photos: Andrew Priestley
Writing Matters Publishing
Website: www.writingmatterspublishing.com

ISBN 978-0-9956051-6-9

Dedication

This book is dedicated to all those who take on the
exciting challenge of starting a new business;
and to my coaching clients for allowing me
to share their journeys.

Contents

At a glance

Starting! is appropriate for entrepreneurs thinking about launching a new enterprise; and ideal as a review process for any established business that is under-performing or at risk of stalling.

Popular business reality TV shows like *Dragons' Den* (UK) or *Shark Tank* (USA) encourage hopeful entrepreneurs to pitch their business concept to a panel of successful, seasoned investors. The panel of experts ask probing questions about the viability of the business. Contestants either walk away with cash and a high profile business partner or they leave empty handed.

Viewers often watch these shows for the entertainment value of winners and losers and many marvel at the experts' ability to quickly assess each business opportunity.

But how do they do it?

Firstly, the process typically requires participants to submit the *Executive Summary* of their business plan. This assumes they have a written business plan. Presumably, researchers then review the submitted *Executive Summary* for strengths and weakness and subsequently brief the panel of experts who then - on-air - ask questions to clarify anything not clear or covered in the *Executive Summary*.

Importantly, their questions are not random or guesswork because they are asking business plan-type questions.

Starting! explains these key *business plan-type* questions.

The questions are easy enough to understand, explained with theory and then supported with relevant case studies.

The reader learns how to identify assumptions in their business case; and tests those assumptions for flaws.

Importantly, given the high global failure rate of start-up businesses in the first 12-24 months, the questions are well worth answering *before* you launch your business.

Entrepreneurs are encouraged to answer these questions to better predict challenges and therefore the chances of success and failure before trading commences.

Don't start?

Starting! visits the harsh reality of business failure but gives entrepreneurs a proven approach to unpacking their idea for a business. Importantly, it helps them to identify and stress test any assumptions that might inhibit success.

Please Note

The author has clients worldwide and uses £, £ and €.

All case studies are used with permission but names and business types have been changed to protect confidentiality.

Award-winning business coach, author and speaker

Andrew Priestley is an award-winning business leadership coach, qualified in *Industrial and Organisational Psychology*.

He is a best-selling author, speaker and is listed in the *Top 100 UK Entrepreneur Mentors, 2017*.

Starting! draws on over 27 years in business and 18 years working with start-ups and established business owners in a broad and diverse range of industries.

His previous book *The Money Chimp* is a #1 ranked book on *Amazon* for money management.

**Part 1
Think like an entrepreneur**

STARTING!

Jumping off bridges

When I was a kid growing up in Australia, the summers were sweltering hot so my friends and I used to ride our bikes down to the river, near the golf course, to go swimming.

The riverbank was lined with towering, ancient ghost gums and from a massive overhanging bough someone had strung a thick rope that us kids used to swing out high over the river before flinging off into the cool water below.

One day I saw a much older boy do something amazing. He jumped off the small bridge that spanned the river. Curled up into a tight ball he created the biggest explosion of water I have ever seen. When he emerged seconds later he was greeted with enthusiastic cheering and whistles.

So I decided to jump off the bridge, too.

The bridge didn't seem that high until I had climbed up onto the top railing. Suddenly, it seemed a very long way down and I instantly regretted my bravado!

But with all my mates now cheering me on I realised I had painted myself into a corner. So I climbed the rail and steeled my self to jump.

Just as I was about to jump a golf course ranger came running along the bridge waving his arms and yelling, "Hey you! Kid! Get down off the rail!"

Grabbing my arm, he hauled me off the railing and back to the footpath.

"Can't you see the sign? No Jumping Allowed? It's not safe. You've gotta be careful! It's too dangerous."

Here's the thing. Starting a business is just like that. You've got a great idea and you're keen to get going. It looks risky but you want to go for it. But then along comes someone like me – business consultants, accountants, experts - who tell you to slow down, look before you leap, read the signs and above all be careful.

The truth is starting your own a business is amazing. You should start your own business because it is exciting and can be incredibly rewarding.

But the truth is it is also risky.

You can easily get into trouble very quickly because you were in so much of a rush and so keen to get going that you ignored sensible advice like, 'Do some research. Do a small business course. Write a business plan before you start your business. Make haste – slowly.'

And given the high new-business failure rate within the first 12-24 months that advice makes sense.

So I'm predicting – at first - you might not like this book because it seems to say, 'Caution! Slow down. Play it safe. Don't start a business - yet!'

But stay with me because each chapter will make you a little bit smarter, a bit wiser and importantly, a lot clearer about what makes a business succeed in the long-term. Good advice that will pay off.

Specifically, it's designed to help you unpack your business idea so that you end up with a solid business case, hopefully a business plan that makes commercial sense if you choose to write one but importantly, a long-term successful business.

And by the way, did I jump?

Three big lessons for entrepreneurs

Entrepreneurs are known for coming up with good ideas. And they want to turn those ideas into a successful business. If this sounds like you then you are in the right place.

The problem is while you might have a good idea for a business you want to be sure you have a good business for your idea. That is mission critical because too many new businesses fail within the first 12-24 months. Invariably, the idea is good but the business supporting the idea, isn't.

There are *lots* of things you can do to ensure you turn your business into a successful business. But in my experience there are three things that absolutely must happen:

1. You need a good plan, preferably in writing.
2. You need to carefully check your plan for flaws.
3. You need to make strategic decisions that make commercial sense.

But what I see instead is:

1. No plan, a bad plan or the wrong plan
2. No checking, poor checking or lots of guesswork; and
3. Flawed strategic decisions.

The two recognised factors that drive the behaviour of most entrepreneurs are:

1. Rushing (driven by the fantasy of extraordinary success or the fear of missing out); and
2. Guesswork and wishful thinking.

Most entrepreneurs love ideas and hate planning. They just want to crack on. But statistics are against this strategy. I'm speaking from experience.

Like me, you may have to learn those lessons the hard way.

Big Night Out!

By the way, did I jump off the bridge? Of course I did! I'm a rule breaker. Tell me not to do something and of course I will ignore you. Once the ranger left, I jumped.

For the record, I actually lost my balance and plummeted face first into the icy water. The pain was excruciating.

Did I learn my lesson? No.

I jumped right into my first business, too.

Like most entrepreneurs I got a good idea and I didn't want to wait. I was itching to get going and springboard into action.

When I was a kid I loved to draw and do jigsaw puzzles. I was very curious about how things worked. I did a lot of exploring and in hindsight I did a lot of dumb and even dangerous things like jumping off a bridge – usually to impress my mates.

I once jumped off the garage roof and broke my arm. My mum said, "What were you thinking?"

My dad said, "Top end for think; bottom end for sit."

When I was at university I worked on the student newspaper. I loved the creativity and I really loved the process. I learned how a newspaper was put together. I learned about lay-up pages, galleys, typesetting, sub-editing, bromides and pre-press production.

It was a lot of fun and as a team we had a wonderful time putting out the student newspaper once a month.

After I graduated from university, I got married and

started a job as a schoolteacher. In our spare time my wife Diane, an eager young journalist, and I started an alternative health newspaper called *Vision*. After *Vision* came *Surf City Extra*, a surfing/lifestyle newspaper, and then *The Mix*, a music newspaper.

After ten years of teaching I was entitled to take three months paid long-service leave. I decided to quit teaching and do publishing full time.

So we moved to Queensland, Australia and started a free entertainment newspaper called *Big Night Out* (BNO!).

It covered the Brisbane pub music scene and included a comprehensive gig guide. But it also included jazz, folk, indie and classical music as well as fashion, food, movies, theatre, art and culture. And that made it unique.

When *BNO!* burst onto the scene it created an instant buzz. It was fresh, quirky, well designed and innovative. At its peak we had most of the major players in the entertainment and hospitality industry buying loads of ad space. And that got the attention of our mainstream competitors because we were making a dent in their advertising revenues.

So far so good, right? At first it seemed like an exciting idea. But I am going to confess I didn't write a business plan or do any major market research.

But I did have what I thought was a good idea for a business. And it was. But I didn't have a good business for the idea.

I did every single job involved with publishing a newspaper. I sold advertising, wrote content, took photos, did the design and layout, did the paste-ups, the sub-editing and the pre-press production.

I delivered the artwork to the printer, helped them create the printing plates, sat there and watched with pride as each issue came freshly minted off the press and then loaded up the car and drove back to the city to distribute each new issue to our growing network of pubs and clubs.

Incredibly, *BNO!* grew rapidly in page numbers and circulation but so too the costs, the overheads and the wage bill. It quickly became a victim of its own success.

It voraciously churned through all my long-service pay and after two months, we were almost out of money. So we took a bank loan of $25,000, which then disappeared equally as fast.

The fun was very short-lived. It lasted about a week or so.

BNO! quickly consumed every waking moment demanding 12 to 16 hour days, seven-day weeks. After six months, I was burnt out and making dumb mistakes.

Diane had a background in working with a dynamic team on a daily regional newspaper and was keen to hire specialist contributors. I relinquished editorial control to focus on production and let the staff write whatever they wanted. The paper disintegrated into a dog's breakfast. One guy wrote a social column and wanted pages of social pictures of five star events. Another was writing long-winded, two-page historical pieces on defunct bands from the sixties. Another was writing controversial pieces on social issues. And another was writing about the emerging Indie fashion scene. We stopped having editorial meetings and focused on filling pages. And I was too tired to care. Lay out, print, layout, print.

Subsequently, the quality dropped and the readers stopped taking the papers. Pubs then started throwing away issues and asked to be taken off the circulation.

Worse, the advertisers were confused and ad sales started to fall away. As the ad sales declined the page count dropped even further and each issue got thinner and thinner. And the cycle tightened and worsened.

I made very dumb decisions like placing last minute, full-page advertisements without contracts with clients who didn't or wouldn't pay their invoices.

In the end I was giving away ad space. Our last issue had 12 pages. But I knew it was unsustainable long before the last issue.

So one gloomy Friday night, I made the decision to pull the pin on *BNO!*

But by then I hated it. I was exhausted, we were broke and it nearly destroyed my health, our marriage and family life. But frankly I was relieved it was over. I just wanted it to end.

I closed the office and used what was left of the business loan to pay out staff and my creditors. Everything was gone - the offices, the staff, the equipment, the computers, the desks, the vehicles.

Everything, except the bank debt. It took another five years to pay off the business loan for a business that no longer existed.

So what did I learn?

Lessons learned

Looking back I learned what *not* to do. If I distill it right down, it comes down to three important factors:

- **Spend a lot of time on your plan preferably *before* you start trading.** Get it out of your head. Talk about it. What *exactly* is your idea for the business? What do you *see* happening? Take your time and go into as much detail as you possibly can. You should write a business plan eventually – and I encourage you to do that because there are several very good reasons for doing so – but start by exploring how you see your idea working. Flesh out your idea in as much detail as possible. The exercises in *Parts 4* and *5* will help you do that.

- **Next, stress test your plan for assumptions.** Every plan – and really do mean every plan – always has assumptions, some obvious and some not so obvious. Assumptions like what? OK, you are assuming your idea will work. You're assuming there is a demand for your products and services and a long line of paying customers and of course they are gagging to buy. You're assuming they are easy to find and reach. You're assuming you'll make money. Some untested assumptions are annoying but benign.

Others will sink your business and may cost you a lot of wasted time, effort and money. This step is all about removing guesswork and replacing wishful thinking with reality checking and diligence and *Part 5* will help you do that.

- **Importantly, think like an investor and make strategic business decisions.** And I mean decisions that make commercial sense. If you do the workshop in *Part 5* thoroughly you might discover flaws in your plan that need to be addressed. You might discover that even though you've got a good idea, the business is not worth doing just yet, or at all. A good decision might look like *not* starting the business unless and until you have resolved those issues through more planning and stress testing. *Parts 4* and 5 will give you case studies about people who successfully revised their plan; and some who didn't; and what happened next. The choice of course is yours, but choose well.

Starting! gives you a proven method that has worked for a lot of entrepreneurs worldwide. I am quietly confident it will help you turn your good idea into a good business, too.

Lessons applied

I learned invaluable business lessons from my business failure. A failure is a failure if you learn nothing from it. I reverse engineered what failed and importantly I put all of that experience and hard-won knowledge to work in my next business.

This is important, because this book is not worth reading at all if you don't apply what you are learning.

Fortunately, we were young and resilient enough to recover from our first business failure. My next business idea was a marketing agency for small businesses.

I wrote a business plan – nothing fancy - but at least it was a basic plan to follow.

I read books, listened to CDs and attended business courses. I learned about marketing, management, operations and finance. I spoke to accountants, joined business networks and connected with successful business owners and inspiring mentors.

We weren't a big agency and didn't charge big agency prices. I built a customer base on our *nice-price* marketing service focusing on a catchment of local businesses within a 25-mile radius.

BNO! taught me a lot about advertising - what works and what doesn't - so I focused mainly on print (newspaper, *Yellow Pages*, magazine, handbills, brochures) and a small amount of electronic (radio and TV).

I knew that most small business owners struggle to create effective campaigns, communicate their value or come up with compelling offers.

I was good at copywriting – both short and long copy ads - something I learned to do running *BNO!* I was also very good at helping clients A/B split-test and measure their marketing efforts to identify the offers that generated the most wanted response like increased footfall.

Most business owners I talk to today *still* don't test or measure anything in their marketing.

I helped clients communicate value through handbills, brochures and booklets.

I was invited to write a marketing advice column in the local newspaper and even mentored several small businesses helping them achieve between 30 and 400 per cent uplift in revenues through marketing.

Even though I had a profitable little business my biggest competitor offered me a well paid, account executive role, which at the time was a good career move and an offer too good too refuse. It was nice to earn a big salary, stop worrying about money and to step back from business ownership for a while.

Over 18 months, I helped increase sales revenues from $350,000 to $1.8 million and got to work on some large campaigns. For example, a campaign for a major property developer sold $6 million worth of waterfront land in two hours, which made front-page newspaper and evening TV news.

I helped double the footfall of a natural health food supermarket – one of the first in Australia. I created a special end-of-season, closed-store sale that netted over $23,000 in sales in one day – an inconceivable result for a small handicrafts retailer. Our letterbox campaign trebled local visitation for a major tourist attraction. In all cases we aimed to find and leverage the hidden value in the business.

Subsequently, we won several prestigious industry awards.

Drawing on my own experience running a business, we focused on business development issues and improved our own marketing and sales; resolved internal management, administration and staff issues; reduced costly operational inefficiencies and dramatically enhanced the quality of financial reporting.

Some of my clients noticed these improvements to our own business and started asking 'business development' type questions. *"How did you do that? Why did you do it that way? What would you suggest we do?"*

Clients would discuss their business frustrations and I'd make suggestions and happily they paid off.

As a result in 1998, a friend suggested I would make a good business coach. "What the hell's a business coach?" I asked.

When I started, business coaching was an emerging industry. After quite a few detailed discussions, I left the agency and started as a business coach, which I have been doing ever since.

When I started the emphasis was business development with a clear focus on strategic direction; business performance - driving revenues, growth and profit; improving operating efficiencies; and raising staff productivity. Those four pillars still underpin the work I do with clients.

Over time I added business leadership development because I started to notice that some business owners were the hand brake on their own success. People say work on the business but I worked on the leader working on the business. When I coached the leader, the results were amplified and the results showed up bigger and sooner. Subsequently, over several years I've shifted my focus from business development to developing the business leadership skills and abilities of the owners.

Fast forward several years and I completed my degree in Industrial and Organisational Psychology, won several industry awards for coaching, wrote two #1 ranking business books and in 2017 was listed in the *Top 100 UK Entrepreneur Mentors*, which was a thrill.

Outside of my own coaching business, I am the head coach for *Dent*, an international entrepreneur training company founded and run by my brilliant son Daniel Priestley and his savvy business partner Glen Carlson that operates in six cities located in UK, Australia, Singapore and the USA.

The dynamic *Dent* team works with established entrepreneurs with a desire for business success aiming to solve meaningful problems in the world.

In my capacity with *Dent* I mentor the *Threshold Accelerator* that helps early stage SMEs take their revenues through HMRC's £83,000 value added tax (VAT) threshold.

Starting! distills what I have learned over many years from successfully working with a broad and diverse range of industries and businesses.

The truth about entrepreneurs

Every entrepreneur I meet sincerely believes they have a good idea for a business and just like me with my lifestyle newspaper idea; entrepreneurs are usually keen to jump - no - *springboard* into action.

But while you might have a good idea for a business, you need to be sure you have you got a good business to support your idea.

IDEAS   PLANS   STRATEGY

Most entrepreneurs do not commit their ideas to a written plan. The old adage is true: *if you fail to plan, you plan to fail.* When an entrepreneur tells me they have no plan I can reliably predict they will waste time, effort and money and the business will struggle to wash its face, as the saying goes.

Rarely do they *stress test* the *assumptions* embedded in their idea.

The truth is *every* business idea contains assumptions - things you genuinely assume to be true; and *want* to be true. These assumptions need to be identified and carefully checked.

In my experience, very few entrepreneurs devote any time to stress test those assumptions. I think secretly they fear the idea will not stack up so it's better not to look.

Usually the idea is brilliant. The problem is almost always you don't have a good business to support and drive the idea.

Subsequently, the venture is not grounded in commercial reality and that probably explains the high rate of new businesses failing within the first 12-24 months.

Starting! is designed to help you explore your business idea; and identify and stress test the assumptions that underpin it.

There are in fact three functions you need to fulfill.

- The *entrepreneur* comes up with *good ideas.*
- The *business owner* comes up with *good plans* so the business will deliver value to customers.
- And the *investor* comes up with a *good strategy* by checking the plans carefully to ensure the business delivers a return on your investment in time, money and effort.

Entrepreneur, business owner and *investor.* Three different ways of thinking.

The truth about good ideas

Want to know the secret to being a successful entrepreneur? Come up with good ideas.

Specifically, entrepreneurs look for *a gap in the market, an emerging trend* or *an emerging industry*. And that's where entrepreneurs get most of their good ideas for a business.

Critically, you must solve a clearly defined problem for a target customer or niche and have clear proof that a minimum viable market exists. That's the business end.

Often you will be improving on an existing idea. For example, *Apple* did not invent the MP3 player but the *iPod* was an industry changing improvement.

Believe it or not the first electronic handwriting device was called the *Telautograph* patented by Elisha Gray in 1888. Handwriting recognition was invented in 1957 and for sale by 1964. By comparison, *Apple's* first tablet the *Newton MessagePad* was a latecomer in 1993.

Newton was superseded by the *Palm Pilot* (1996); the *Intel Web Tablet* (2001) and then the *Microsoft Tablet PC* (2002). *MessagePad* was resurrected in 2007, included touch screen technology and rebranded as the *iPad*. It was successfully relaunched in 2010 and has gone through best-selling iterations ever since.

Apple didn't invent touch screen technology either. That's been around since 1965. Nor did they invent multi-touch, pinch and resizing which was invented by the mid 1980s and commercially available by the mid 1990s.

But while *Apple* didn't invent any of these innovations they saw the gap, the trend and the emerging industry and are the world leader in mobile devices!

My point? Rarely will you come up with a new idea or innovation. Most entrepreneurs take an existing idea and improve, innovate or simply import what's already there. The key is to spot an emerging trend, a gap in the market or an emerging industry

The three owners of *Starbucks* imported the barista style coffee service and flavour options they'd enjoyed in Europe to the USA and the rest, as they say, is history.

Emerging trends always represent massive opportunities. For example, the post-war *Baby Boomer* generation started to turn 70 in 2016.

The *Boomers* have created entire industries linked to the changing needs of their natural aging process. When the *Boomers* were born there was an increase in products for babies, then toddlers and young children.

When the *Boomers* became teenagers, the growth markets were in music, fashion and entertainment and when they became adults who wanted to own cars and houses. Now as they start to age and retire the emerging big trends are in finance and health services. But I've noticed an emerging industry in retirement coaching.

Millennials on the other hand are the antithesis of the *Boomers*. They want instant gratification and convenience but don't want to own anything!

This has spawned companies like *Uber* and *AirbNB* who have flourished because they leveraged that emerging trend.

So in most cases you do not need to come up with anything new. You might make a lot of money by improving what already exists but always by looking for a gap in the market, an emerging trend or an emerging industry.

For the record, *BNO!* wasn't new.

When I lived in London in the late 1970s, I read *Time Off* and saw the emerging trend of the *30-somethings* who had more time and disposable income to spend on leisure activities and tourism driven by the desire for a more globally connected cosmopolitan lifestyle.

At the time the music press was rock and roll not lifestyle. So I spotted an emerging trend and a gap in the market. There was nothing like that in Australia so I *imported* the concept.

So while *BNO!* was a fresh take – it was nothing original. But people wanted to read our newspaper and our competitors started to copy what we were doing.

But be clear: my new business didn't fail because of the idea. It failed because the idea didn't have a good business to support that business idea. My business idea was jam-packed with untested assumptions that I chose not to explore.

And I refused to slow down and write a plan. I was excited and in a big hurry to start. I discovered almost immediately that I didn't know how to run a fast-growing business with so many complex moving parts.

So while its great to spot a gap in the market, an emerging trend or an emerging industry it's worthless if you can't leverage those insights or you court failure because you refuse to do basic planning and concept checking.

I had the idea but I wasn't thinking like a business owner. Like most entrepreneurs, I was bullet proof and I didn't think my idea would fail.

STARTING!

What's Failure Rate?

It's important to discuss failure. The cold truth is far too many new businesses fail. Depending on whom you listen to – governments, the taxation department, banks or business experts – most new businesses fail within the first five years.

The *UK Parliament* (2015) says that one in four new businesses fail within in the first 24 months.

Based on the failure to lodge their first self-assessment, *HMRC* pegs that figure closer to 50% whereas *Companies House* puts it closer to 70% within the first 18 months.

Banks and business experts are less generous and say that eight in ten new businesses fail within the first 12 months.

CLASS OF 2012 ··· 12 MONTHS LATER

In 2012, The *London Evening Standard* profiled 100 bright and shiny, promising start-ups. Twelve months later 98 of them no longer existed.

But whatever the percentage, 25%, 50%, 70% or 80%; or the time frame of 12 months or 12-24 months, or five years, the failure rate is too high, especially if it's *your* business. You don't want your new business to fail, right?

But if you shirk planning and stress testing, statistically, you will not be the *exceptional case* where failure happens to *other* entrepreneurs.

In 2015, 608,111 new business started in the UK. That was 50,7675 new business start-ups a month or 1,666 a day!

If 80% of those businesses ceased trading that equates to 486,488 or 40, 540 a month or 1,338 a day!

By the way, was the economy the factor? Was business failure more prominent during the *global financial crisis* (2007-2014)? Not really. These failure rates have been fairly consistent for over 60 years in both boom and bust.

I read a great business book in 1980 called *Bigger Profits in the 80s* and it was citing similar stats back then.

Failure *still* comes down to a lack of planning or flawed plans which, sadly, are reliable predictors of early stage failure.

You need good ideas but you need a solid business case to ensure success. Preferably, you don't start a business until you have a solid business case.

Why did my business fail?

My first business failed within 12 months. So what happened? I have studied reasons for business failure for many years and here is a list of general reasons that by now might seem obvious. Pay attention if they already resonate.

I was in too much of a rush

In my experience, most entrepreneurs I meet are in a mad rush to start their business. Like most entrepreneurs I was keen to get going, too. I thought that a good idea was all I needed to succeed. Wrong. Business experts have been urging us for over 50 years to slow down, err on the side of caution, plan, launch conservatively and execute slowly.

The big message is slow down.

I didn't have a plan

54% of new business start-ups still don't have a written plan. We know this from studies into loan applications for bank finance.

There was a time when you could apply for bank finance for a business loan without a business plan. All you needed was a profit and loss statement. But since the global financial crisis of 2007, those days are over. Today you must have a business plan especially if you want business finance. So, write a plan.

My plan was flawed

Banking studies tell us that 96% of business plans that accompany a loan application are flawed. Banks are looking for a clear strategy and a solid business case that makes commercial sense. Most plans I read have gaping holes in the business case that clearly suggest the plan wasn't checked. So check your plan carefully.

I couldn't sell

Here is the best piece of advice I will give you in this book. Most entrepreneurs think a good idea is all they need. They imagine a queue of customers lining up with credit cards or cash in hand and a gagging need to buy. They start the business and then discover they actually have to go out and find customers and start selling. The truth is 95% of your focus needs to be on selling and 5% on the idea.

BNO! relied on paid advertising and it didn't take me long to realise that my real business was sales. But I couldn't sell.

So, I hired a guy who claimed he could sell but he couldn't either. He blamed the economy, the industry, the pubs and clubs, the record companies and the punters. Everyone but himself.

Most entrepreneurs I meet struggle with sales. Your business relies on sales revenues, so learn how to sell.

I was under-resourced

Most entrepreneurs I meet are usually punching well above their weight and of course, under-resourced.

BNO! actually competed with the *Courier Mail,* Brisbane's mainstream daily newspaper.

Newspapers have many moving parts that require journalists, photographers, designers, sub-editors, typesetters, printers, sales people, distribution, financial control, accounts etc. I took on all those jobs and in pre-digital days that involved laying out a newspaper by hand. We wrote editorial, took photos, did pre-press typesetting, bromiding, design, layout, design, sold ads, designed ads and even loaded the printing plates onto the press. Plus I did the invoicing, bookkeeping, the ledgers, paid suppliers, wages, the tax ... and ... and ... and.

It was just the two of us running a business that needed at least 30 staff. And even when we eventually employed about nine full and part-timers we were still under-resourced.

So who do you need on your team?

I didn't know how to run a business

Having a business idea is very different to running a full-time business. Business guru, Michael E Gerber describes this succinctly in *The E Myth*.

An *entrepreneurial seizure* is where the people who are good at doing the technical work believe they can *successfully run a business that sells that technical work.*

I could do the technical work but I'd never run a business before. I'd never read a management book. I made it up on the spot. And that *still* describes most start-ups I encounter.

There were too many problems

Businesses are a problem magnet. Don't ever imagine that success brings fewer problems. The more successful you get, the more problems you will generate.

One key assumption is you will be able to handle whatever the business throws at you. Statistically you won't.

The good news is, if you can survive the first two years, you will become more skilled at anticipating and solving business problems.

I had no idea how business finance works

This is pretty much a cliché for start-ups. Far too many new business owners lack any grasp of the commercial reality of running a profitable business. The assumption is finances will take care of them self. They won't.

Newbies tell me they have a great month of sales but then can't understand why there's no money in the bank.

I knew I had to make more money than I spent. But I didn't understand basic bookkeeping or taxation. I didn't know what a balance sheet or P&L was or how to read them. There were no revenue or cash flow projections.

I only knew I needed to sell enough advertising to cover the production of each issue. Never mind about making a profit. I know that *BNO!* turned over money but it went straight back out again. But I honestly could not tell how much money *BNO!* was making or losing. Most start-ups have no clue on what performance they want, could or should expect.

And that is the key problem I see almost every day. So, learn about business finance and financial control.

The business did not deliver
the intended benefits

Why did you start your business? This is a critically important question for every business owner to answer honestly.

Understand, at the heart of it, you assume your business can deliver more lifestyle benefits than paid employment.

I started my business to provide a better lifestyle for my family but it did not deliver lifestyle benefits to my family.

My business did not make us money. It cost us money and then lost us money. And it left us with a debt that took five years to repay. So, be clear. What *exactly* are the benefits you want your business to deliver?

Of course, this list is not exhaustive but the key themes relate to your plan, checking the assumptions in your plan and making sound business decisions. *Starting!* will help you address these three key issues.

But the biggest reason I failed is I didn't think like a business owner. So, if the job of entrepreneur is to come up with ideas, the job of the business owner is to come up with a workable plan.

No such thing as 'all of a sudden'

The purpose of a plan is to succeed but also it's to anticipate and mitigate predictable problems. The big lesson I have learned is: in business there is no such thing as *all of a sudden*. You almost always get a heads up about problems. Honestly, you don't go to bed one night, wake up the next day and discover that your business has *all of a sudden* failed overnight. Rarely ever does it work like that.

In 2001, *Ansett Airlines* was Australia's major carrier with the lion's share of the domestic aviation market. In the early hours of September 14, 2001, *Ansett* went into liquidation and was placed into hands of the administrators. A stunned Australian public woke up to discover their favourite airline was not only grounded but closed for business.

Management feigned surprise but the problems were neither recent nor hard to spot.

In fact, as the story started to unravel it became apparent that the writing had been on the wall for some time.

Big or small, there are four key places where problems show up in *any* business - including yours (*see p167*). They are:

- marketing and sales;
- management and administration (and HR);
- operations (logistics and IT); and
- financial control.

Ansett had problems in those four areas.

If you are handling problems in those key areas you can predict success. If you are ignoring those problems you can predict difficulties and failure.

Ron has financial control issues. He has customers who take over 120 days to pay their bills. This creates a constant cash flow problem that Ron carries via his overdraft. Ron doesn't charge late fees so in effect there is no consequence for late payment *and* he is giving his debtors an interest-free loan.

Even if you haven't started your business, is it possible to anticipate potential problems that will undermine the success of your business?

Yes. If you want to borrow money from a bank or an investor they will ask questions designed to help them assess whether you are a good lending risk or not. To do that they will ask to see your *business plan.*

The problem is most business plans contain unsupported and therefore flawed assumptions.

For example, when a start-up says they will capture two per cent market share, I am curious as to how they will achieve that. That's an obvious example of an unsupported assumption.

This suggests you think like an investor and check the assumptions in your plan, too. Which makes sense because you are the prime investor in your business, right?

So maybe you should ask yourself the same questions a bank or an investor might ask, to see if you are a good risk!

Part 2
Think like a business owner

STARTING!

Should you write a business plan?

Of course you should write a business plan but this book is not about writing a business plan because there are already plenty of excellent business planning books and resources available.

Starting! is about identifying and stress testing any key assumptions in your business case *before* you write your business plan.

The standard business plan has two purposes:

a) to help raise finance; and/or
b) to help management make strategic decisions.

Raising finance

In most cases, you'll write a business plan to secure funding from either a bank or an investor. When I was running out of operating cash I needed a loan to keep trading. Basically, I prettied up the P & L statement, sent it to my bank manager and he approved the loan.

Most people rarely refer back to their business plan once they have the finance approved. Likewise, I promptly put the plan in the bottom drawer and never looked at it again.

Strategic direction

The second reason to write a plan is to provide strategic direction to the management team even if that's just you.

However, entrepreneurs rarely write a business plan to provide strategic direction. Ironically, this is exactly what you should do!

The key questions I always ask entrepreneurs are:

1. Why are you starting your business?
2. Will your business deliver the intended results?

BNO! delivered results but not the results I intended. I didn't realise that, successful or not, a business is consuming cash especially if it's failing! And more so if there's no plan. And I didn't have a plan and worse, didn't think I needed one.

When I ran out of cash in 1990, the bank was happy to lend me money. They asked me to submit a business plan with my loan application so I was finally forced to write a business plan.

But here's an important question: is it your *choice* to carefully plan ahead to ensure you have a business that will succeed? Or is it your *duty* to ensure you have the best chance possible for success by having a business plan that makes good commercial sense - no matter what, regardless?

This is a shared philosophy of Sarah-Anne Lucas, author of *It's Never About the Fitness,* and early stage SME expert, Robin Waite, author of *Online Business Start-Up.*

They would say it's your *duty* not a *choice* to plan for success.

You may think you can start a business without a plan but all that changed in 2007.

The world really changed in 2007

In 2007, the *Macquarie Bank* in Australia started to closely monitor the sub-prime mortgage delinquency crisis in the USA, and quickly changed its lending requirements. They started to demand more skin in the game from borrowers.

By 2008, the lending practices of banks and companies like *Fannie May* and *Freddie Mac* had apparently triggered the global financial crisis which resulted in six to eight million delinquent mortgages.

More than two million US homeowners lost their homes.

Countless companies went bust, many downsized and thousands of workers were made redundant. Many found new jobs and many of those who didn't decided the only option was to start their own small businesses.

And new business start-ups have spiked since 2007.

Small business accounts for about 65-75% of all new jobs created in the US while home-based micro-businesses account for 53% of the small business sector.

In the 2009 US census, businesses with less than 20 employees made up 89.7% of the workforce.

In the *UK House of Commons Business Statistics* reported (December 2015) 99% of businesses are small to medium sized businesses employing less than 300 people. 95% of those are micro-businesses employing less than 10 people.

Small business accounts for a third of national employment and 18% of national revenues.

Startupbritain.org tracks *Companies House* registrations. Start-ups have grown steadily from 440,660 in 2011, to 608,111 in 2015.

But up to 80% of these registered new businesses fail to lodge a taxable self-assessment within the first 18 months and so technically they are either under the taxable income level and therefore under-performing financially; or they have ceased trading.

To get a different perspective we look at bank lending.

Banks have money to lend to businesses but since 2008 banks have focused on bank-ready, investor-ready businesses with a very solid business case and significant cash equity.

By 2010, banks were insisting on a solid underlying business case.

A business case is your commercial justification for starting your business in the first place designed to convince a decision maker - usually a banker or an investor - to lend or invest money. Naturally, your business case has to show how sustainable revenues will be generated, how you will generate an attractive profit and return on investment (ROI) and your growth plan.

Of course, they want to know if you can repay the loan.

Banks work on the principle that any fool can lend money – the trick is getting it back. At a bank forum in London, 2012, banks indicated they were definitely thinking twice about lending to what they termed *zombie* businesses - businesses that fail to grow; and exist only to service debts or a loan.

This means if you want bank finance your business better have a solid business case and a plan based on something more solid than wishful thinking. Because most inexperienced start-ups find it hard to estimate the future earnings and performance of their business the end result is usually a work of fiction and therefore flawed.

Once upon a time, all that was needed to get a bank loan was half-decent profit and loss statement (P&L). Now banks want more than financials and sales projections; they want your strategy.

The question is: if banks and investors want solid answers to these questions, why don't you?

54% of start-ups have no written business plan

According to banks 54% of new business start-ups seeking finance have no written plan. I was advised by some very savvy business people to write a plan but I started my business without one. I just wanted to crack on.

If I had written a plan for *BNO!*, I am certain I would never have started that business. I think this might be why most entrepreneurs avoid planning. They don't like the thought that their idea might not work. In any case, there is just no excuse today to start a business without a written plan.

- There are literally thousands of free or low cost business-plan websites on the internet.
- *The Princes Trust* (UK) has an impeccable, free, plain English, user-friendly business plan template perfect for entrepreneurs.
- There are any number of free or low cost business development courses.
- Your bank most probably has online business planning resources as well as phone and face-to-face advisory services.
- Your local authority probably offers free business advisory services.
- There are countless business coaches, accountants and business advisors offering business-planning services.

So the big lesson here is: write a business plan. This advice has not changed in over 60 years.

But once again, this book is not about writing a business plan. This book is about identifying and then stress testing the assumptions in your business idea *before* you write your business plan.

Why do I care? I care because business failure usually comes with a high price tag. The average small business failure loses £19,000, the typical mid size failure loses £37,000 and SME failures lose on average £82,000. That's non-recovered money.

My first business cost me $38,000.

If any business fails I know money is involved.

Remember it took me five years to trade out of my bank loan paying of a loan for a business that no longer existed! I could have declared bankruptcy and absolved my debts. That was an option. But I didn't take that route.

Imagine if I'd borrowed that money from family or friends. I know families that have invested their lifesavings - usually their pension pots - hundreds of thousands of pounds - into a business started by a family member, that failed.

Relationships rarely recover from that.

And yet despite the persistent eight-in-ten business failure rate, most entrepreneurs still feel they don't need anything more than a good idea based on a best-case scenario and wishful thinking.

96% of business plans are flawed

I met with the CEO of Business Lending for a major UK bank who told me that while he had seen a dramatic upswing in business planning since 2008, his research showed that 96% of business plans that accompany loan applications were flawed and subsequently, did not received funding.

Alex wrote a business plan. His business plan says he wants to borrow USD$67,000 so he can purchase a container load of superseded cell phone handsets (currently in a warehouse in London) and ship them to a country in Africa where their current retail value is USD$400,000.

Sounds a good idea, right?

The plan says he will ship them from the UK to the African destination, find a reseller and then sell them. According to his plan there are cell phone resellers lining up to get their hands on that shipment.

Have you already spotted any flawed assumptions in his business case, so far?

For starters it is assumed that he could actually get the stock out of the UK. His plan does not mention export duty or import taxes, storage, customs, insurance required in the UK and elsewhere. There's a reason those handsets are banged up in a warehouse gathering dust.

He doesn't mention that the target country is landlocked. There are no are no docks. But his plan said he intends to send them via container ship because he cannot afford to ship the consignment by air.

He has to get them off the docks in either Mozambique or Tanzania and truck them overland. His plan mentions nothing about clearing customs, excise taxes or complex issues in crossing borders, delays, quarantines, embargoes etc.

Critically, while he has a list of resellers for the handsets there are no contracts or paid pre-orders. The plan is to get them there first and then find resellers and then start selling. The plan says he will sell them but doesn't say who to exactly.

His plan fails to mention that he has no experience in exporting, whatsoever. Nor has he consulted someone like *UK Trade and Investment*.

The problem with most plans is they are based on unsupported and untested assumptions – maybe not as dramatic as this - but still capable of causing headaches for the over-eager entrepreneur.

When the bank, not surprisingly, declined finance, Alex started to ask relatives to invest in the project offering generous *Returns On Investment*. The assumption is his plan would work but it seemed his relatives were skeptical, too.

On paper this looked like a fast way to make money.

In reality it was a financial disaster waiting to happen. Yet, like a true entrepreneur, he pushed on with his 'plan'.

The reality is the majority of business plans do not stand up to even the most basic stress testing.

Most *plans* are: *'Everything will go really well according to plan, there will be customers, I will sell a lot of stuff and make a lot of money.'*

On the face of it, Alex produced a textbook business plan. What he didn't do was explain or test the assumptions in his plan. In a sense, he focused on writing a plan but cut corners on critical thinking.

I am urging you to think like a business owner and unpack your idea. Carefully identify and stress test any assumptions in your idea for a business *before* you write your business plan.

Starting! shows you how. I'm wondering if you will?

Success in 80 Days

By 2009, I was totally convinced that entrepreneurs needed to write a business plan and that plan had to make commercial sense.

Banks convinced me that without a business plan entrepreneurs stood little chance of achieving funding especially if the plan that accompanied the loan application was flawed.

I also knew that venture capitalists (VCs) in particular have a highly developed sense of whether a business plan is viable or not, just from reading the *Executive Summary*. They have the uncanny skill of spotting unsupported assumptions.

I worked with an experienced business investor, David Robson, to develop a way to identify flaws in business plans.

We created a comprehensive programme for stress testing a business case called *Success in 80 Days*. It took two to three months to go through a business plan with a fine tooth comb but the result was business case that would pass close scrutiny by a bank or seasoned investor.

In 2010, we ran a series of workshops but only a handful of delegates signed up for the full service.

We discovered that entrepreneurs hate planning. They agree that planning is a good idea – *for someone else!*

We also discovered entrepreneurs do not want to pay for a plan critiquing service! They saw it as a *grudge* purchase.

While the lack of interest was disappointing the handful of clients who did go through the full *80-Day* process emerged with superb plans and enjoyed success that far exceeded expectations. One client pivoted from one idea to a much better idea, and two others decided not to start the business – for the right reasons.

David did however, find a willing market in government clients who understood and appreciated the value of thorough planning.

But despite obvious benefits, entrepreneurs stayed away in droves.

80 days down to 90 minutes

Entrepreneurs repeatedly asked: *"Why does it take so long? Is there a shorter version of the 80 Days process available? Can you do this in 90 minutes?"*

The answer is no. You cannot condense the value delivered in a comprehensive 80-day concept-checking process down 90 minutes and get the same outcome.

But I developed a snapshot version that takes 90 minutes. What emerged was the 90-minute *Business Strategy*. And it is an invaluable pre-business plan tool.

While the snapshot version is not as thorough or comprehensive as the full-blown *Success In 80 Days* programme, it still delivers immense strategic clarity and direction and highlights exactly where detailed attention is required.

And like the full version, it flags flaws *and* opportunities.

In *Part 5*, I'm going to teach you exactly how to run your own 90-minute business strategy session.

So what have you learned so far?

The *entrepreneur* comes up with the ideas. So if you want good ideas think like an entrepreneur.

The *business owner* comes up with plans. So if you want a good plan think like a business owner.

The *investor* checks the commercial strategy. In which case, think like an investor.

And that's where we are going next.

STARTING!

Part 3
Think like an investor

STARTING!

Can you lend me $25,000?

If the job of the business owner is to plan, the job of the investor is to think strategically and make sure the plan will perform.

Seasoned bankers and investors have the ability to quickly spot the assumptions in even the best-looking business plan. So after they read your business plan they usually ask cut-through questions intended to stress test any underlying assumptions in the business idea.

To give you a sense of this process, imagine if I came to you and asked you to lend me $25,000 for my business. I am assuming you'd ask me a lot of questions. So what questions would you ask me?

Seasoned investors ask questions like:

1. Why are you starting this business?
2. What's the idea for the business, exactly?
3. Who's your target customer; and why them; and what problems will your business's products or services solve for them? Do they want your solution?
4. Who's on your operating team? Who do you need? And why?
5. What is your route to market and is there proof that a minimum viable market exists for your idea ?
   Who's already doing what you're doing?
   Who are your competitors?

6. What will you sell? How much?
7. Is your business – financially - worth doing? What are your costs? Margins? Sales forecasts? Profits? Have you thought about an investment, equity or exit strategy?
8. What is your business model? Is this a boutique business or is it scalable?
9. What systems and process do you need to run your business smoothly? Any IP issues?
10. How will you know it is working?

Business plans tend to focus on the financials but they are usually based on best-case assumptions that the business will run according to the plan. The questions above aim to identify and stress test assumptions that underpin the financials.

They go beyond financial performance and look for factors that might impact overall business performance, which is why they are so useful.

Is your business ready for investment?

This might seem an odd question for a start-up, but is your business ready for investment? I don't mean is your business in *need* of investment? I'm asking if your business could actually *attract* investment funding.

Funding comes in two forms a) bank finance such as a bank loan, personal loan, second mortgage, overdraft, line of credit and b) non-bank finance such as professional investors, venture capitalists, angel investors etc.

Bank Finance

Bank finance usually requires some form of security such a personal guarantee attached to something like a second mortgage on the family home. In the past the bank was not that interested in your business idea – they were more interested in your ability to service the debt and make loan repayments for the term of the loan.

Since 2008, banks are shying away from businesses without a written business plan. They can quickly assess if you are proposing a *zombie* business that will not grow and exists only to repay the loan.

Non-Bank Finance

Non-bank finance is no different. Professional investors expect a solid business case and they expect greater results above and beyond what a bank would expect. And on top of that they expect a solid ROI, equity or an exit valuation.

If you are serious about succeeding then, big or small, you should aim to be either *bank-ready* or *investor-ready* for three key reasons.

Firstly, writing a business plan for a bank or investor is an excellent way of clarifying your thinking about your business, which is why it is highly recommended.

Secondly, if you do need finance you will be ready!

Thirdly, you are the primary investor in your own business.

So start thinking like an investor capable of spotting flaws in the plan that will inhibit growth and a healthy return on investment. This is especially true if you used whatever life savings you have as seed money and working capital.

And especially true if you have borrowed against an asset like your home.

So, how do investors think?

Dragons and Sharks

In 2005, the BBC launched a new business show called *Dragons' Den* based on the original 2001, Japanese TV show of the same name. *Dragons' Den* spun off into *Shark Tank*, the USA version. Different names but the format is the same.

Entrepreneurs - usually SMEs, inventors and manufacturers - pitch their business ideas to a panel of wealthy investors - the *Dragons* (or the *Sharks*). They want financial investment in exchange for an equity stake in the company.

What is fascinating is just how quickly the *Dragons* decide whether they want to invest or not.

Of course, every entrepreneur thinks they've got a great idea for a business. I've never met an entrepreneur who thinks they have a bad one.

As you'd expect, the *Dragons* ruthlessly strip away the hype and relentlessly stress test the idea for commercial reality. They turn up the heat on turnover, gross profit, costs, margins and net profit. And within 12 minutes they have either opted out and occasionally opted in. Just like in real life where 80% of businesses fail, 80% of pitches end up with no investment from a *Dragon*.

And for a while I wondered: how do they decide whether to invest or not so quickly? Do you need years of experience and qualifications to think like a seasoned investor? Or is this a skill anyone could learn? I think you can develop the skill.

If you apply to appear on *Dragons' Den* you have to submit the *Executive Summary* of your business plan.

No surprise then that the *Dragons'* ask *Executive Summary*–type questions. And that's what seasoned VCs do, too.

My friend David once skim-read the *Executive Summary* of a plan but quickly rejected it.

I wondered: "What is he looking for exactly?" So I asked, "What was wrong with the plan? Why did you reject it?"

He said something like:

- I didn't know why they were starting the business.
- I didn't get the business concept. It wasn't clear.
- I didn't know who it was for - exactly - or why.
- I wasn't convinced they had the right team.
- I wasn't sure a market exists; or how they intend to go to that market.
- I'm still not sure what the core offering is.
- The numbers don't seem to stack up.
- The business model seems wrong.
- I can't see how it can be scaled.
- There's lots of moving parts but no operational plan or documented systems and processes.

So let's look at one of the plans I reviewed recently:

"I want $50,000 to create an e-commerce site to help emerging artists sell their paintings to collectors who look for emerging artists ... usually pieces for around $2,500 ... artists will list their artwork and collectors will buy artwork from the website ... $25,000 will be used to hire a web designer ... we will drive traffic to the site via *Twitter*, *Facebook* ads, *Google Adwords* and via PR ... artworks will be shipped to customers via *UPS* ... we expect to gain 1% of the market ... we project revenues of $250,000 in Year 1 ... ."

Reread the above excerpt a couple of times and decide if you would or wouldn't invest in this business.

If you would, why? If you wouldn't, why not?

From what I've seen so far, I wouldn't be investing. I've seen enough. For me there are already far too many assumptions.

I might be wrong but if a piece of art starts from $2,500 – unless it's a really well known artist - I don't think collectors will buy online unless it's someone they really trust, like *Sotheby's*. I'm not sure if *Facebook* ads or *Adwords* will sell paintings.

I imagine collectors would buy from a gallery but I could be wrong. But that doubt is making me doubt the plan.

I don't think you can get a good web designer and a great e-commerce site for $25,000

I am immediately doubtful of the claim that he will gain 1% of the *art market* in Year 1, or what 1% of the *art market* even looks like. It's not clearly explained.

Sheldon has a well-intentioned idea but unless something radically changes this doesn't *feel* right or like a good business to support his idea. Right now this *feels* like a recipe for stress.

My guess is Sheldon has rushed the writing of his business plan. I'm sure the plan makes sense in his own mind, but right now it's not standing up well to a even quick stress test. I think most entrepreneurs are scared to stress test their business idea in case they discover the idea won't fly.

They are emotionally invested in it working and when that gets questioned they take it personally and get defensive. I bet you know people who have stubbornly refused to let go of a what *feels* like a bad idea.

But bankers and investors *do* test your assumptions … and they *do* start crosschecking … because they *do* want a business to work … because if it's their money … they *do* want a return on their investment.

And by the way, so should you! You should be just as diligent as any savvy investor. If not, more savvy.

If you look at enough business plans you develop a horse sense for a good and a bad plan. At a gut level, the plan either feels right or it feels wrong. Usually if it feels wrong it *is* wrong.

If I were pushing business plan writing I'd encourage you to first read lots of business plans similar to your business. They are easy to find on the web if you look. Reading business plans should be your new hobby!

When I've queried seasoned investors about a plan that didn't *feel* right they would usually raise similar concerns to the one's David listed. Importantly, as soon as it feels wrong, they start looking for reasons to reject the plan outright.

And here's a heads-up: seasoned investors simply stop reading at the first flaw they come to! They think: *If this is wrong then what else is wrong?*

And if it *feels* wrong that usually means no investment funding.

The business strategy workshop included in *Part 5* gets you to think like an investor in your own business. You will be surprised at just how quickly you spot the assumptions in your business idea once you start answering questions.

Even if you don't have a written business plan yet, you should use the workshop in *Part 5* to explore your business idea more thoroughly. Stress testing and crosschecking takes time. That's the downside.

But the upside is a much stronger business case.

Part 4:
Stress testing the idea
for your business

STARTING!

Ten business success questions

Each year I read many business plans and conduct hundreds of face-to-face business strategy sessions for both start-ups and established businesses, but plan or no plan, I can quickly tell if you have a solid business case.

Your business idea should cover these important themes:

- Your big why
- Your business concept
- Target customers
- Operating team
- Route to Market and Sales
- Product ecosystem and price points
- The Numbers
- Business Model
- Systems
- Review

Stress testing covers these broad themes.

There are hundreds of questions that you can ask to stress test a business case but over time I've noticed they segment into ten broad themes.

Ask yourself the following questions and make notes. Importantly, note how these questions make you *feel*.

And notice the questions can you answer easily and the questions you are worried about or avoiding answering?

- Why did you start your business?
- What exactly is your business idea or concept? Is it clear?
- Who is your target customer? Why them?
- Who is on your management and operating team (internal and external)? Why them?
- Is there proof that a minimum viable target market exists; and what is the intended route to that target market?
- What will your core offering/s be? What will you sell? For how much?
- Do the numbers stack up? How do you know your business is worth doing?
- What is your business model? Why that one? Is it a boutique or scalable business?
- Are your systems and process documented?
- Will this business deliver work/life benefits?

Even brief answers to these questions start to clarify your business case. I'm encouraged if I hear clear answers to these questions, but I'd be worried if:

- I have no idea why you started this business.
- I am struggling to see why you are even bothering with this business in the first place.
- Your business concept isn't clear enough or at all.

- It's not clear who the target customer is - exactly - the key problem they've got or the problem your product or service solves. It's undifferentiated.
- Your business seems under/over-resourced people-wise. I have concerns about your management and operating team.
- You haven't demonstrated that there is actually a viable, profitable target market (or customers) for your business or a clear route to that market.
- It's not clear what you sell - your core offering - and for what price.
- The numbers don't stack up so
- You don't seem to have the right business model. Your idea doesn't seem scalable.
- You don't have documented systems and processes.
- The business is all-consuming or is shaping up to be like that.

In *Part 5*, I want you to answer these questions. But right now, let's explore each of the questions in a little more detail.

Question 1:
Why exactly did you start your business?

You need to give this question a lot of careful thought.

Why do you want to start your own business?
Or: why exactly *did* you start your business?

It might surprise you, but far too many people do not have a clear answer to this question. Many will say, *'For the money. To be my own boss.'* Answers like that.

But dig deeper. Go for more substance and depth. If you are going to pour a ton of time and money into your business, it's worth taking the time to think of the key reasons why you started one. Once you start your business you won't have much spare time for reflection because you'll be too busy; most likely too busy working hard for the wrong reasons.

So deep dive into that question.

Some Common Reasons
This list is by no means exhaustive but here are some typical answers.

To use my qualifications, skills or expertise
I'd worked on a newspaper at university. I loved design and layout. And I loved the creativity of print publications. I had a skill set and I wanted to use those skills.

For fun/pleasure

I thought *BNO!* would be fun. I thought it would be fun to create a music newspaper for people my age that loved the music scene. And it was for a short while.

To make a difference

I wanted to make a difference. I had been to London and read *Time Out*. I'd seen the sophisticated music press in Paris and Los Angeles and loved what they did with design and layout.

I wanted to shake up lifestyle press. I wanted to see my peers sit up and take notice.

Big Night Out! covered a lot more than just rock'n'roll. It included jazz, opera, theatre, fashion, art, food, travel, and events when the entertainment papers focused purely on the pub culture. It was eclectic, funky and eccentric and the punters loved it.

I developed good relationships with record companies especially *Sony, Warners* and *Universal*, and showcased established big-name performers but I also wanted to give editorial space to new acts that rarely got a look into mainstream press. I am proud that we broke a few acts and even inspired a major music festival called *Big Day Out*.

I wanted to make a difference to Brisbane's cultural scene.

Maybe you want to make a big difference via your business. That puts you in good company.

Dame Anita Roddick of *Body Shop* fame used her success to campaign against the testing of cosmetics on animals; and championed *FairTrade* who aim to give farmers and workers in Third World countries a better price for their products and labour.

Dent's charter is to use their success to solve meaningful problems. For example, they have raised a lot of money for *WaterAid, Peace One Day* and *The Hunger Project*. Our business has sponsored children who would not have received a basic education without sponsorship.

If you want to be a good corporate citizen please align your business with a charity or choose one of the *United Nations' Global Goals* and support their *#GlobalCitizen* programme.

For the lifestyle benefits

A successful business is a great way to create a satisfying lifestyle - nice home, nice cars, holidays, time off and an idyllic family life. I believed my business would help me achieve those outcomes.

I quickly discovered the irony of running a successful lifestyle newspaper that demanded 24/7 attention!

BNO! required me to visit grimy, grotty pubs and clubs smelling of sweat, cigarette smoke and stale alcohol.

The ultimate wake-up call was when the owner of a night-club set an appointment for 2 o'clock to discuss advertising. I remember it was a sweltering hot summer's day and I drove an hour into the city, struggled to find a car park, walked eight blocks and arrived at this nightclub only to discover it was shut! I rang the office and the secretary explained: "No, you don't seem to understand. *The meeting is for 2am, tonight!*"

I drove home stunned. When I told my wife she was dumbfounded. "Andrew, you're seriously not thinking of driving into the city for a business meeting at 2am!"

It was crazy and I didn't go. I finally realised that my business was running in direct opposition to my values.

Around this time a colleague asked me a profound question:

What benefits do you want your business to deliver?

My business goal was to provide a nice lifestyle for my family. I imagined a *sunny Sunday afternoon* lifestyle: family barbecues, lazing by the pool with money in the bank account. However my business didn't deliver this lifestyle.

A client wanted a business that allowed him to go snowboarding ten days at a time, twice a year. His business delivers that outcome and no wonder he loves his business.

Another client wanted his business to sponsor children in need. His company has sponsored over 1,500 orphaned children in Africa for over 26 years.

So you need to think about this carefully. What lifestyle benefits do you want your business to deliver?

Be clear about what you want. Don't just say 'I want a better lifestyle.' Be specific. You need to know because your business will make demands on your time , your personal life and your money. It might clash with your values, if you let it. You need to be clear what you are in business for. Will my business give me more family time? How much time? Holidays? Where? When? A nice home? What sort of home? Will it deliver work/life balance? And if your goal is money, how much money?

Remember: *you* run your business. *It doesn't run you.* If you discover the business is running you, then you are doing it wrong. I learned that big lesson the hard way.

I want to make the money for myself

You must read Michael E Gerber's best selling business classic, *The E Myth*. Here's why.

Let's say you are an employee. You work hard for a boss, and like most employees you don't think you're paid enough. You see how much money clients pay and you see your boss making most of the money.

Then you think, "If I worked for myself I could be making that money *for me*, instead of my boss. Why don't I start my own business and *pay me,* instead of him?"

Gerber calls this moment an *entrepreneurial seizure*. It's the moment when you *decide* you should become your own boss and work for yourself instead of someone else.

But the problem is while you might have the technical skills sold by that business you might not know how to run a business *that sells those technical skills.*

And Gerber says this blind spot is at the heart of business failure.

But people brush this fact aside, and start a business anyway. And almost immediately the problems start. And then you realise life was a lot simpler being an employee!

The problem is, if you have taken a loan, leased premises, and employed staff you are now highly committed to making the business work. You now have skin in the game and the business demands you *stay* in the game. And that is how your business starts running you.

So, you really do need to analyse why you want to invest so much time and money into your business.

- Sheldon, is a painter, and is frustrated that the galleries make more than he does. Yes, his e-commerce site will showcase artists, and make them more money, but he wants to sell more of his own art, as well.

- Early in Neville's engineering career he was working on a mining site and a vehicle caught on fire and sadly the two drivers perished. Neville decided he could design equipment that would protect life. His fire suppression systems are safe, rigorously tested, ISO rated and insurer-friendly. And they save lives.

- Roger is a pharmacist who worked in the family-run business. He saw how much his dad struggled to compete against the major discount pharmacies. He saw declining revenues and spiralling costs drive their independent pharmacy to the brink of collapse. Fortunately he was able to reverse that crisis through improving operating efficiencies, a patient-centric service and the smart use of technology. As a result he now consults to other independent pharmacies and helps the little guy compete with the big players - a true *David and Goliath* challenge.

So consider why you want to start your new business.

But, how will you know you're on the right track?

Mike Harris, is the creator of three UK billion pound entities, and best selling author of *Find Your Lightbulb*. He says, *"It lights you up."*

Importantly, when you explain your big why to potential customers it lights them up, too. If it fails that litmus test you have more work to do.

There is one last point to consider.

If you have a partner, a wife, a husband, a girlfriend, a boyfriend or a significant other - importantly - *does it light them up?*

If your partner cannot see any sense in what you're proposing, slow down. That lack of support will be the cause of ongoing friction and conflict. You owe it to them to answer this question carefully. Don't rush this.

You might have the best-intentioned idea that your partner does not appreciate fully. Don't try to force your partner to get on the same page if they don't share your enthusiasm, yet.

If you are already trading this activity is especially relevant because your *big why* may have changed and the business no longer lights you up. If this is true, then definitely spend more time on this question.

Don't move on from this activity until you have a clear, compelling argument for starting your business and authentic reasons that light you up and inspire you to action.

Your turn

What insights did you get from this section and importantly what are some key actions steps?

Question 2:
What exactly is your business idea or concept?

I perform about 150 business strategies every year. In a business strategy I ask the client to *clearly* explain their business idea. Most can't.

The financier JP Morgan would not invest in a proposition that could not be clearly explained *and* understood in under five minutes. And that's most VCs and angel investors I know.

I ask my client to elaborate on how they came up with their business idea. The ideas that turn into good businesses find a gap in the market, an emerging trend or an emerging industry *and* solves a clearly defined problem or problem set. And there is proof that a minimum viable target market exists.

Sheldon told me that he was an artist - a painter - trying to sell more of his own artworks. By chance, he sold a couple of pieces on *eBay*. He knew *eBay* makes money in listing fees and sales commissions.

When he helped a mate sell a painting on *eBay* he earned a nice commission and it occurred to him that perhaps he could make money helping other artists do the same. Then he thought, why give that money to *eBay*? Why not build his own website and make the money for himself? This is Gerber's *entrepreneurial seizure*, right there.

But can you see how the business came about? And can you feel why Sheldon is already excited about his idea?

Sure Sheldon needs to elaborate on how the business works but for now he needs a very clear and concise idea description of what his business will do.

"I specialise in helping emerging painters to sell their artwork online to collectors; and help them achieve higher than expected sales prices so that ultimately they get the recognition they deserve."

The litmus test is how you would answer the question: *what do you do?* The key is to be clear and concise.

"I specialise in selling select paintings online to discerning collectors."

When I work with clients I spend a lot of time helping them refine their pitch. Just remember if you're unclear or confused then your prospective customer is going to be even more confused. If they are confused they are uncertain. And if they are uncertain they won't buy.

You will know if you're on the right track when other people can clearly explain what you do, and you agree with them.

Your turn

OK, what insights did you get from this section and what are some key actions steps?

Question 3:
Who exactly is your main customer?

This question requires some careful thought. Who is your main customer? Your perfect ideal target customer? Is this someone you already work with or is this a new customer segment or niche with whom you like to work?

Your ideal target customer must meet five criteria:

- You like them and you know a lot about them.
- You can get a great result for them.
- They can afford you.
- They can afford to implement what you are suggesting.
- They refer you more target customers.

Your target customer needs to tick all of those boxes. Don't fall into the trap of saying, *I want everyone.*

THIS IS FOR EVERYONE AGED 9-90

You don't want everyone. Unless you have an ironclad plan for low price/high volume/mass distribution, trying to service everyone is not a good strategy. You'll go broke.

This is why discounting doesn't work. Most new businesses think they will discount and under-charge their way to success but that's a fast track to business failure. At the heart of it is a lack of basic research or a failure to articulate your value.

Do your homework. Gather *demographic* information such as gender, age, occupation, income, buying habits, average transaction value and purchase frequency. And gather *psychographic* information and understand why they buy, what problems they want to solve.

Understand, target customers spend more money, more frequently and over longer periods of time. They require less work and they refer customers just like themselves.

The trick is to be specific. Niche down.

- Kelly specialises in portrait paintings of prize winning, breeding bulls. Her clients are serious cattle breeders who usually have $180,000+ invested in a breeding bull that has sired generations of prizewinning cattle.
  Proud owners want a portrait of the prize winning bull.
- Fiona only paints highly detailed, botanical artworks. She is represented by a specialist agent who sells into the profitable botanical, art market.
- Suzie specialises in boudoir paintings for high net worth executive women over 40.
- Casey, a skillful sculptor, only sells monumental, large-scale sculptures for public spaces and corporate foyers. If you go to his website that's all you will see.

To clearly identify your ideal, preferred target customer, perform a customer or an industry analysis.

Kevin, an accountant, performed a customer analysis. His ideal target client turned out to be a husband and wife operating a family run, service-based business i.e., plumbers, carpenters, painters etc.

They earn about $250,000 pa but want to grow to about $500,000 pa and he can help them achieve that goal.

That segment represents only 16% of his total client base but represent about 67% in billables.

He now bases his entire value proposition around the family run service-business niche. His marketing only talks about husband and wife family run businesses. So who do you think shows up? Who responds to his marketing?

You can be even more niche.

- Darian, an accountant, narrowed his whole offering right down to creative agencies. If you are not running a creative agency he won't accept you as a client.
- Mick, an accountant, only works with premier league footballers with property holdings greater than £10 million.

The key to niching is ensuring there is proof that a minimum viable market exists. If you're unsure who your target customer is and what specific problem the product or service will solve for that specific client type, you're in trouble.

So who exactly is your ideal target client? Who do you really want to work with? Why do they need what you're offering? What problem does your core offering solve for these people? Another way of exploring this question is to ask: *What is the outcome you want for that customer? Or what do they really get when they work with me?*

You might also ask: *Who don't I want to work with? Who wouldn't I want as a customer?*

For example, I don't work with bankrupts.

I've found if a business is turning over less than £300,000 per annum I know they will usually struggle to implement major game changing recommendations. They understand why I am making the recommendation but lack the wherewithal to follow through.

I recently suggested that a client invest in cloud based accounting. That meant transferring a lot of data across from their offline accounting packages. But they did so at a big investment in time and money. That recommendation is already reaping efficiencies, savings and dividends.

I worked with an agri-business who specialised in irrigation and plumbing supplies. They had over 36,000 *stock keeping units (SKUs)* stored in their warehouse.

After a stock take and sales analysis they discovered that 20% of their specialist stock items generated 73% of revenues; 35% made up the next 24% of revenues; and 45% of slow selling stock items made up a minuscule 3% of revenues which Peter had stocked *just in case.*

But that 45% of stock took up nearly 50% of their warehouse space! Basically, it was costing them money to stock those items. He sold off those items, which freed up a lot of space and importantly freed up a lot of money that was tied up in dead stock.

Greg ran a timber yard for fencing contractors. Customer analysis revealed that his contractors spend on average £500, £1,000, £1,500, £2,000 and £2,500 a month.

Guess which fencing contractors routinely pay their bills late, cause the most headaches and want the best deals? Right, the £500 and £1,000 per month customers. Guess which ones are the easiest to work with and are the most profitable? Right, the £1,500 - £2,500 customers. So why give those lower paying clients the same benefits offered to the higher paying clients?

Greg discontinued offering trade terms to late paying, low-end accounts. With no loss in income Greg offloaded most of his low-end accounts and now happily *over-services* his high-end repeat business accounts.

This question alone deserves a lot of thought because it will impact your bottom-line if you get it right - or wrong!

You will know you're on the right track when you can clearly explain who your ideal target client is.

Your turn

OK, what insights did you get from this section and what are some key actions steps?

Question 4:
Who is on your team?

Seasoned investors focus on the three Ms: *management, management* and *management.* Importantly, they examine who is on your operating team and the quality of those people.

You need to think carefully about your operating team. Do you employ staff or is it just you? Or do you have casual or part-time staff? Or outsourced sub-contractors? In any case, what roles do they perform? What responsibilities do they have?

Maybe you don't need to employ a team? Maybe you can fully outsource all aspects of your operation, offer flexible team delivery and act as a coordinator or project manager.

I know of a law firm that manage large legal-medical contracts but employ only two people. They assemble pre-gelled, flexible delivery teams of sub-contractors that can deliver the specifications of the project.

You also need to see your suppliers as a part of your team. Your *team* includes anyone you need to help you deliver a result whether they are on the payroll or not.

In whatever way your operating team is composed, there are four main functions within any business that require team member input - *marketing and sales; management and administration* (and include HR in this function); *operations* (and include systems, logistics and IT) and *financial control.*

Those roles need to be performed by someone with skills, knowledge and abilities.

If *you* are the business – a one-man band, *'solopreneuer'* - doing the work of a team, then there's a high likelihood you will be spread too thin.

When we started *BNO!* we didn't realise that effectively we were in competition with media mogul, Rupert Murdoch. He owned the *Courier-Mail*, the major daily newspaper in Queensland.

The popular broadsheet included a lavish lifestyle section, produced by a *Features* department, which employed 35 staffers. And it needed that many people because a lifestyle magazine has a lot of moving parts. When we started *BNO!* it was just two of us, punching well above our weight.

As I outlined in a previous chapter, I did everything. I wrote copy, typeset it, did the design and layout, took photos, scanned photos, sold advertising, created the ads, proofed the copy, wrote the invoices, chased payments, paid the bills and much more.

I had what is called a *1/3, 1/3, 1/3 business*. A third of my time was spent getting the business, a third was spent doing the operation of the business and a third was spent managing and administering the business. When I was getting business, I wasn't doing the operations. When I was doing the operations I wasn't doing admin or sales. No wonder I was exhausted!

Sheldon is a *'solopreneuer'* and his business will be 24/7/365 e-commerce, platform. Running a 24/7 e-commerce website has multiple moving parts.

And an e-commerce site requires a team. I think Sheldon has underestimated just how much is involved in running a successful ecommerce site. And how long it will take to get it working.

A client started an e-commerce site that was supposed to take three months to be up and running. Two years later it is still not finished and to date has cost over £150,000. So this kind of business venture needs a lot of thought.

But you still need the right people. So, who do you need on your team?

Your team is made up of your *internal* team (people on full, part-time or casual salaries) and your *external* team like sub-contractors and suppliers - people who help your business succeed.

You might include other professional service providers who partner with you on a project to ensure your clients' needs are met. But I also include your accountant, your lawyer, your insurance agent, your IFA as well as printers, couriers, and even service providers such as power, phone, internet, water and the postal system.

In a workshop I give delegates a huge piece of paper and get them to list everyone - and I mean *everyone* - they can think of that supports the business. If you do this activity you will be surprised at just how many people hang off your business.

I have 180 people that *touch* my business in some way.

So once again: Who do you need on your team? Who do you need to make sure your business succeeds? You need a complete and clear picture of who you need on your internal and extended team.

Your turn

This is an important question, so what were your insights and key actions steps?

STARTING!

Question 5:
What is your route to market?

This part of the business strategy is all about your marketing, finding customers and making enough sales to justify starting the business.

When I started *BNO!* I was confident that a market existed. There was a vibrant hospitality and entertainment industry in our city.

My route to market was personal selling. My sales aids were a business card, a brochure and a rate card. I drove round to all the pubs and clubs and sold them ad space. I knew how much ad space sold for in competitor newspapers so I simply undercut those prices!

Market research is so important. Most entrepreneurs do minimal research, and lack proof that a minimum viable market exists. There is usually no marketing plan, no sales/revenue projections, no indication of the size of the market and no competitor analysis. But they start anyway.

As an example, Sheldon had managed to sell a couple of his pieces on *eBay*. He also sold a few pieces for a couple of fellow artists and made some small commissions for his effort. He concluded that he should create an e-commerce site that sells artworks for other artists.

That sounds exactly like me when I started *BNO!* I had skills in laying out newspapers and made the major leap into the idea that I could start a major city entertainment newspaper! *How hard could it be?* People want lifestyle and entertainment news, right?

The obvious flaw was entertainment newspapers are usually free. So my *real* customer wasn't the punters but the hospitality industry. Did they want another advertising vehicle when there were already four entertainment newspapers touting for their business?

I didn't know but I went ahead started the business *anyway*.

Of course I was greatly encouraged when I signed up my first customer. The mistake I made was thinking a small win was a solid commercial argument for creating a full-blown business.

If I did that business today I would *float* the idea first. I wouldn't try and sell anything. I would look for *expressions of interest* and *signals from the marketplace* that there was sufficient interest to proceed.

I would write a brochure and go visit as many target prospects as possible and elicit their feedback and support. I'd make sure the concept was at least minimum viable.

As a start-up, you must prove that a market exists; how you will reach and engage that market; and clearly demonstrate how you will achieve the forecasted revenues.

If you are convinced a minimum market exists and you have a route to that market then you will also need a sales plan and a sales process.

If you are going to start a business you'd better make sure you know how to sell because even if a minimum viable market exists success will depend on your ability to enter that market and make sales.

I have a client who does leadership training.

Staff training is a lucrative market but usually you have to become a *Preferred Supplier* to get work. But getting on the *Preferred Supplier* list is a lengthy and arduous process. And even if you can get on a *Preferred Supplier* list there is no guarantee you will get the opportunity to quote on training projects.

So 'minimum viable market' means minimum viable market for *your* business. Yes, a massive market might exist but it's worthless if there are *barriers to entry* that inhibit your ability to enter that market.

Many would-be business people have an excellent business concept but terrible marketing. In most cases they lack a cohesive marketing strategy that identifies the optimum route to market. You may need to engage a marketing expert to perform a marketing audit to determine the best route to market for your business.

And you might have good marketing but you can't sell.

I know people with a great business concept, a great offering, a big market, and minimum viable market potential for their business who will *not* pick up a phone. They literally sit waiting for the phone to ring.

Colin bought a franchise that sells social media campaigns for local, high street retailers. It's a proven concept. It works. That's why a franchise exists. Colin paid £24,000 for that franchise. His franchise fees contribute towards a local marketing campaign designed to raise awareness. But you still have to do your bit and go out and engage the market personally.

In two years he has sold £1,200 worth of social media campaigns because he doesn't like selling. And he says he can't sell. A minimum viable market exists but he won't phone, canvas or cold call his local high street retailers. Somehow, he hopes, they will discover him and sell themselves!

The ability to sell might be the only thing holding you back. That's why it might be helpful to assess your sales skills.

I created a profiling tool called *The Sales Profile* to do just that. The ability to sell is made up of *skill* and *will*.

If you distill effective selling there are ten sales skills: *readiness, knowledge, prospecting, rapport, qualifying, presenting, closing, objections, service* and *administration*.

And there are three drivers - attributes that moderate the skills. For example, the *drive to succeed in sales* is a primary driver of success in frontline selling.

Here's what our study shows: People with high will and low skills typically *outsell* people with high skills and low will!

Someone with drive and enthusiasm can outsell a skilled but demotivated sales person. If you need to sell it would be handy to know your strengths and weaknesses in selling.

The Sales Profile is therefore a very handy test to take because it shows you exactly where you need help.

Take *The Sales Profile* test at:

www.thesalesprofile.com

It measures your strengths and weaknesses in tens skills and three key attitudinal measures associated with high performance in a front line sales role.

You are on the right track when you can prove there is a minimum viable market for your product or service, you know how to reach that market through relevant marketing and you can sell into that market.

Your turn

OK, what insights did you get from this section; and what are some key actions steps?

Question 6:
What do you sell? How much?

What are you going to sell and how much will you charge? *BNO!* was a free newspaper that relied on advertising sales. I had to go out to pubs and clubs and sell ad space. For the first issue I calculated the costs involved and sold enough to cover those costs. My pricing model was undercut the rate card of my competitors in order to win a customer.

But I didn't factor in wages, rent, electricity, taxes and other overheads. So make sure your pricing structure covers your fixed and variable operational costs and that you are charging appropriately so that you make a profit. Otherwise why are you doing this business?

Sheldon believed he would sell the artworks at a lower price than galleries but this means he would have to sell in higher quantities to cover his costs.

Too many start-ups charge a small price in the hope of winning customers but most people don't realise that if you have a cheap price and low volumes you sacrifice margins, don't make a profit and inevitably go broke. Cheap is OK if you can sell in high volumes but low prices and low volumes won't generate sufficient revenues or profits.

When I eventually put up the prices of our ads a lot of my *loyal* customers wouldn't buy because I had educated them to expect low prices!

So you will need to explore the relationship between what you sell, the price and viability. A business plan will require you to set some targets and do a sales forecast.

In hindsight I would have done a lot more competitor research especially on rates and charges, looked very closely at my costs, looked at my margins and profit projections and then decided if the market was viable and if I wanted to enter that market.

I recently worked with a personal trainer who was charging £40 an hour for a training session. I did a basic cost analysis, and quickly determined that he actually needed to charge £75 for an hour.

We worked out that the typical average client does ten sessions over a three-month period, spending £400 in total. We revamped the offering, bundled in some added value such as massage, diet and nutrition, image consulting and yoga and charged £3,000 - basically £300 per session. My client pays £50 for those other value-add services and now averages £250 per session.

I got my client to stop selling his time for money and start selling value-packed packages and retainers. Now he sells £3,000 programmes and is building a viable six-figure business.

If you sell time for money or an hourly rate you need to appreciate that what you deliver and what the client gets is so much more than an hour of your time. This question is not just about price but perceived value. Most entrepreneurs fail to articulate the value they offer and wonder why they don't have many high paying customers.

Your product ecosystem

In our *Dent* accelerators we teach entrepreneurs to create a *product ecosystem*. A product ecosystem lists everything you sell ranging from free, then lower price items right through to your core offering. It's your sales funnel but it is also a logical progression of offerings that makes sense to your customers.

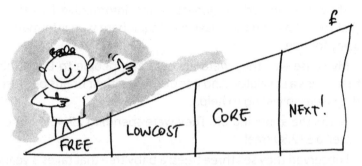

Your customers are going on a journey so it may as well be one that leads them to your core products and services. Instead of having a bunch of unrelated products and services you organise your offerings into a logical sequence so one thing leads to the next. That's why it's called an ecosystem.

Below is an example of a product ecosystem for a plant nursery that leads customers to the core offering.

Free	Low Cost	Core £1000+	Next £3000+
Website	Merchandise	Garden design	Garden tours
Social media	Books, seeds,		of the UK,
Blogs	tools, compost,	Full landscaping	Europe, USA etc
Tweets	soil testing	services	
Facebook Posts			
Free Reports	Paid workshops		
Open days and	Plants		
free workshops	Low cost £12+		
Advice clinics	Mid range £35+		
	Expensive		
Garden club	£120+		

In the example above the husband and wife horticulturists were specialists in Acer trees a wonderful ornamental tree that has a huge fan base in the gardening world.

When I visited the nursery I noticed they went to great lengths to offer advice about soil preparation, positioning and plant food to ensure the Acer trees thrived.

They were incredibly generous and informative but all of that took time and they gave all of their hard won information away for free.

My sense was they were encouraging people to DIY a job that needs a specialist. And people picked their brains because they were so willing to help.

Here's the annoying bit. They were spending 25-40 minutes to sell a £12.50 tree!

I observed they sell three trees: a baby tree that takes 3 years to bloom (£12.50); a teenager tree that takes 2 years to bloom (£37.50) and an adult tree that will bloom this year (£120). Which one would you want?

So we created a free report that generally explains the three trees and the information about blooming time periods, soil preparation and placement.

They introduced a garden club and weekend clinics and free and paid workshops. Then they gave information about garden design, landscaping, planting and even tree surgery and local authority planning.

Lastly, they organised coach tours to famous regional gardens and are now planning a European tour.

And the best bit? The average sale went from £47 to £883.

You will know you're on the right track when you have a product ecosystem, and a value based pricing structure and a client journey that makes sense to your target client.

Your turn

OK, what insights did you get from this section and what are some key actions steps?

Question 7:
Is your business worth doing?

Every question relates to creating a minimum viable business. Your business has to worth doing.

So let's start with a basic question. What is the revenue target for your business this year? What's that number? Look at what you sell and the price points and simply calculate how many products or services you will need to sell to hit that target. Simple maths.

I lead the *Dent Threshold Accelerator* in London where the goal is to smash the £83,000 *HMRC* VAT threshold. A business needs to average £7,500 PCM and the fastest way to do that is to create and sell product or service packages and retainers valued at £2,500+ each month.

A personal trainer sold sessions for £40 an hour. Time for money. Now he sells £3,000 packages. Last year he sold 31 packages and turned over about £90,000.

If he were back selling time for money he'd need 225 clients to get the same financial result.

You'll recall that I said a lot of businesses fail in the first 12-24 months. Invariably, these failed start-ups had no clear revenue targets.

This is a critical activity. Some people are good at their job and they think: *"Why am I making my boss rich? I may as well start my own business and pay myself the same money!"* But they haven't got any targets and haven't factored in the costs of *doing* business.

For example, plumbers probably paying an apprentice £12-£15 per hour but charge the apprentice plumber's time out at £75 per hour or five times the apprentice's hourly wage.

The apprentice might think that's not fair but overlooks the need to cover overheads, buy plant and equipment, pay rates and taxes, insurance and so on. Of course, the business owner would be foolish to sell the apprentice's time at the same rate it costs to employ an apprentice.

As a rule charge out rates should be a minimum of 2.5 times the hourly wage rate but I know companies that charge their people out at 10 or 20 times their hourly rate.

My mistake was divide the $2,000 print cost of *BNO!* by 26 available ad spots. Some ads sold for $75 so all I did was barely cover the cost of printing.

Your business has to be worth doing. A key part of any business plan are your financial projections. You have to ensure that you can cover your costs and make a profit. An accountant can help you prepare those projections. Make sure they are conservative - not best-case.

You know you're on the right track when the numbers stack up.

Your turn

OK, what insights did you get from this section and what are some key actions steps?

Question 8:
What is your business model?

Your job is to get your goods and services out of your hands and into the hands of your customers. How you do that is called your *business model.*

You might open a high street retail store that relies on footfall. Or you might be a B2B wholesaler. You might want to take your business online like Sheldon. Or it might be via agents and sales reps. Or a subscription model. It might be a license or a scalable franchise model. Or you might simply sell IP licenses. I don't know what is the best model for your business, but there is one. How do you see it working?

Helen sells hair care products to thousands of women via *Amazon's Fulfilled By Amazon (FBA)* programme. Her business model is 100% global, online e-commerce. While the online platform looks simple, the backend is a global distribution partnership with *Amazon* and China-based suppliers capable of meeting an increasing global demand.

This suggests her business model allows for high growth and is scalable.

Her job is to promote her items, which she does through social media channels. She has a constant stream of *YouTube* videos, and some savvy 24/7 software that drives interest via *Instagram, Twitter* and *Facebook*. Her job is to build *Friends* and *Followers*.

She has a CRM that compiles client data for direct email bundle/unbundled campaigns and of course she has tapped into *Amazon's* purchase algorithm that notes buyer's preferences and suggests other compatible products.

She is especially focused on building her US market, which currently represents 95% of all sales. But her business model is online sales and distribution.

Graeme has a retail and wholesale fencing business that relies on footfall. His business also becomes uneconomical to run once deliveries exceed a 20-mile radius of his lumberyard.

Customers outside of this radius literally lose him money. For example, if he gets a fencing job 20 miles away his truck will do a 40-mile round trip that incurs costs in time, labour and fuel. If he has to drive 25 miles, he starts to lose in the costs of doing business (CODB).

Worse if there are return-to-base issues.

His model is a retail and wholesale model. His plan is to open new hardware shops in nearby regions or find agents that sell his products. So his business model is about replicating his retail model with agents and reps.

Sheldon's website is an online e-commerce site. It's a basic brokerage model, switchboard or middleman concept very much like *eBay* (which incidentally is already set up!)

Essentially this question is all about what you are in control of. Whatever your business, the model will determine how you run that business. And the model determines the viability and profits. Different models have different requirements. A retail High Street store has very different operational requirements to an e-commerce site even if you sell the same items.

My business model is a boutique, service business. I have also created an associate, coach-the-coach model training coaches in my proven coaching methodology to generate additional income. Coaches can use my IP under license and I earn a percentage of sales revenues.

Systems and processes will play a major role in this model's success. I know of a training company that has scaled to six countries through licenses and systems.

You need to determine what is the best model for your offering.

If you intend to scale, a physical retail outlet might not be the best model unless the cost of the retail outlet is covered by the licensee. *McDonalds* uses this approach. A prime real estate location is part of the offering.

Amazon started as a global online bookstore. The little High Street bookstore can't compete in terms of price because they don't have *Amazon's* buying power or volumes. However, *Amazon* cannot replicate the personalised attention you get from your local bookseller. The UK bookseller, *Waterstones* has managed to achieve a level of in-store personalisation and customer care, which allows them to compete against *Amazon*.

If you are in retail competing against large entities like *Amazon* I recommend Archer and Taylor's *Up Against The Walmarts: How Your Business Can Prosper in the Shadow of the Retail Giants (1994)* which will give you an arsenal of proven strategies, tips and advice for creating a hard-to-beat, highly personalised shopping experience.

If you do own a retail outlet you need to offer something much more than just products. You need to create a branded, personalised customer experience that builds repeat business from loyal customers and increased transaction values.

Of course you can't go past Shaun Smith's *Managing the Customer Experience* (2002) if you want to learn more about creating a truly remarkable customer culture.

Jim is a High Street retailer who runs a chain of lighting stores. He knows that retailers today are competing with the huge online competitors like *Amazon*. He noticed that customers would come into his store, get loads of product information, helpful advice and even lighting solutions and then go home and do their shopping online!

He realised he could not compete on price with *Amazon* so he set about re-creating the in-store experience.

It starts with some very simple questions that side-step two issues: *price shopping* and *free advice*.

"We basically became a specialist retailer. We no longer aim to be the cheapest and we longer educate people how to be better on-line shoppers. Now we find out what people want; sell them a solution service; and sell them all the reasons why buying online would be unwise."

He now helps High Street retailers become specialist retailers too. They are heavily invested in rent and long term leases and so it's well in their interest to overhaul their business model to make it more desirable starting with the customer experience.

Whatever model you choose I urge you to download *Google's Winning the Zero Moment of Truth* white paper on online shopping and consumer buying trends and read it at least ten times! I would also read subsequent updates.

ZMOT discovered 84% of American customers now do online searches for products and services, 70% use product reviews and 54% do comparison shopping.

You'll know you're on the right track when your business model is clear and makes total sense in terms of creating a minimum viable business.

Your turn

OK, what key insights did you get from this section? What are some key actions steps?

Question 9:
Do you have documented systems and processes?

Even if you have no intention of scaling your business your job is to run your business as efficiently as possible.

There's an *optimum* way to do anything and whatever you do on a regular basis, therefore, should be documented.

The purpose of systems and processes is to discover the optimum and most cost effective way to deliver value to your customers. That means you avoid time wasting, duplication and superfluous activity, which generates money, reduces costs and saves money.

That's why your business needs documented systems and processes. Any business can benefit from uniform consistency and quality.

If Graeme intends to license or franchise his fencing business he is strongly advised to document the systems and processes before he sells any licenses. That way he has consistency across all stores.

Peter and Neil, run an engineering firm. They have to have ISO quality accreditation as a minimum requirement if they want to bid for tenders or sell engineering services to their target client.

Documenting their quality assurance systems was a huge financial commitment and a time intensive undertaking but the benefit is a consistent quality of service delivery that wins them loyal, target customers.

I worked with a client who sold smart home technology. For a small business, they created impressive installation and commissioning systems to ensure that installations were performed to a consistent high-compliance and safety standard. They earned a reputation for service excellence and it was no surprise that this aspect of the business was well documented.

By the way, those systems were also the backbone of their staff training. Staff members were routinely trained in every aspect of installation in accordance with best-practice ISO documentation.

E-commerce is a minefield of systems and processes and you would be foolish to even imagine running something like that *without* documented systems and processes.

Understand, if your business has systems and processes you actually add massive tangible value to your business once they are in writing. They become assets that add to the business valuation. If you have any doubt, read *24 Assets* by Daniel Priestley.

Helen - remember Helen who sells hair products - has impeccable documentation for almost every aspect of her business. The value to Helen is eliminating unnecessary costs of duplication, incorrect orders, lost orders that result in refunds and complaints.

So the question here is: if there is an optimum way to do everything, what is the optimum way for you to run your business? If your business requires things to be done the right way each and every time is that *'right way'* documented?

The average *McDonalds* store turns over several millions per annum yet each store is run by teenagers with the average age of 15 years and four months. Their parents can't get them to clean their bedroom but *McDonalds* can get them to greet customers, collate orders of burgers, fries and Cokes, upsell customers, serve customers in a courteous way, and deliver service excellence each and every time simply because every aspect of the business is documented in writing.

Importantly, ongoing training, supervision and monitoring is integral to that system working.

Ex-McDonalds, Marianne Page's *Simple Logical Repeatable* is a must-read on systems approach to a business, you cannot go past Michael E Gerber's *The E Myth* or Sam Carpenter's *Work The System.*

If you want a practical introduction to systems design, then you won't go wrong with *Work The System.* Sam operates one of America's busiest 911 emergency call centres. They have a system for answering phones, for taking messages and relaying those distress calls to the appropriate emergency service. Sam's team, simply, cannot afford to get it wrong. They even have systems to prove they responded on time.

A few years back I worked with one of the Australian *Novatel* resorts. Their housekeeping team was made up of itinerant workers; many with language other than English.

A key frustration was the inconsistency of housekeeping. Some rooms were made up beautifully and others weren't.

But the overall frustration was rooms were not ready for standard check-in times for guests.

So we shadowed the housekeepers who were already doing a great job and closely observed they way they cleaned and reset the room.

They still emptied trash bins and replaced linen and towels. They still vacuumed floors and wiped and cleaned surfaces. They still reset the beds, restocked bar fridges and refreshed the bathroom. But they could finish a room in 20 minutes as compared to the worst housekeepers who took

40 minutes plus per room and that did not equate to a better result.

We got them to note step-by-step the way they performed their duties and then taught that method of housekeeping to other staff. And it worked.

Like *McDonalds* we created checklists and work sheets with descriptions and photos (where often the photos were self explanatory enough). Pretty soon rooms were being finished within 20 minutes and they were uniformly excellent.

An air-conditioning business was losing a lot of money on *return-to-base* and *write-off* issues. Basically, the technician forgot parts or equipment, couldn't proceed with the job and had to come back to base. The owner created a system for checking service vehicles *before* they left the depot. That one system has saved them a lot of time and money.

The aviation industry takes this to profound levels. They operate with highly succinct checklists designed to save lives if needed. Highly recommended reading is *The Checklist Manifesto: How to Get Things Right* by Atul Gawande.

Gawande gives an enthralling peak behind the scenes of the surgery and aviation - where clear checklists save lives.

Aren't you glad that a pilot has a four-step process for restarting an ice-clogged, engine that stalls at 50,000 feet? More often than not you won't even realise the engines are turned off! In most cases you are totally unaware that the plane was gliding while you were watching the in-flight movie!

It takes time to map systems and processes but the pay off is exponential. Anything you do in your business has to make or save you money. Systems and processes do both.

You are on the right track when you start developing checklists and documenting your systems and processes that will save you time and money.

Your turn

OK, what insights did you get from this section and what are some key actions steps?

Question 10:
Is your business delivering the intended benefits?

This is technically revisiting *Question 1* but this time you would be reviewing each of the other questions to check what worked and what didn't, what aspects of running your business challenged you most, what lessons you learned, and what is simply unworkable.

But the focus relates to wellbeing.

Karen Ingram runs one of the UK's most successful Pilates training academies. Most of her instructors start a business for lifestyle outcomes. She asks a vital question: How is your life/ work balance? Are you getting down time, holidays, days off? Or are you living, eating and breathing business? If you intend to start a health and wellbeing business her book *Thrive Don't Just Survive* is essential reading.

Your business must deliver benefits apart from money. It must be satisfying. There's not point succeeding financially if your lifestyle or health suffers. Of if it makes you miserable.

So you need to keep checking if the business is delivering the lifestyle benefits you intended. You will know you are on the right track if you feel satisfied with progress. If you still feel excited and enthusiastic about your business.

I was burned out after six months. When we closed the business down I was exhausted but relieved.

The business I have today is a pure delight. I love what I do.

It doesn't feel like work. It delivers a nice lifestyle. I feel happy and fulfilled and believe I am doing meaningful work.

That's your litmus test. It's worth getting it right.

Your turn

What insights did you get from this section? What needs to happen next?

Cross-checking

I want to make an important distinction. In a business strategy I explore each question *individually*. Then I *crosscheck* the information for obvious relationships especially where they seem to conflict with other *elements*.

I'm looking for assumptions. This is what seasoned investors do. How does this element impact that element? If what I'm doing with this aspect is true what does that mean for other aspects of the business?

For example, can you see how *target customer* links to *marketing and sales*? How a good *operating team* might link to your *business model* that efficiently delivers products and services to customers cost-effectively? And how documented *systems and processes* make all of that happen more efficiently?

I hope each of the ten questions has been explained just enough to get you thinking. There are many related questions I might ask in a business strategy but essentially more thought is required if:

- I am struggling to see why you are even bothering with this business in the first place.
- Your business idea isn't clear enough.
- It's not clear who your target customer is, the key problem they've got or the problem your product or service solves.

- You're under-resourced, that is, there is a negligible or non-existent operating team.
- You haven't confirmed that there is actually a viable, profitable market (or customers) for your business.
- It's not clear what you sell.
- You're not sure if your idea is even worth doing, that is, there is no ROI. You don't have the skills and resources to run your business. (Executive Summary questions)
- You don't have the right business model or a cost-effective delivery infrastructure for your products or services.
- You don't have documented systems processes, and therefore no concept of just how big the opportunity is or the ability to scale it.
- The business is making you miserable.

Take a few moments to read this section again until you get a sense you understand each question and how it might relate to the success of your business. It is well worth revising *Part 4* before you do the workshop in *Part 5*.

Part 5:
The Workshop

STARTING!

Before you start the workshop

Just so you get the most out of this workshop, please follow these useful guidelines:

Record - don't write - your answers

Instead of writing your answers, use the voice recorder App on your smart phone and record your answers to each question.

Speaking is a lot easier, faster, more conversational and more natural than writing. Writing does come later, but for now, just record your answers.

When I worked in advertising I used to write long copy ads. I used to record the copy to cassettes – remember them? Then I would listen back to the recording and make notes. Basically, your ears are your BS detectors. If it doesn't sound right to you, it probably isn't right. So record your answers.

Just make sure that your voice recordings can be downloaded to your computer and saved or converted to MP3 files. You might want to get the recordings transcribed later.

It's probably stating the obvious but create a new recording for each question.

Work with a buddy but only work with someone you feel totally comfortable with

There is a certain chemistry in sharing your thoughts with someone else. A friend will ask questions, seek clarification and ask you to elaborate further, and elicit feedback you would have missed when you work alone. That's why I recommend you work with a friend. But choose someone you can trust and feel comfortable with.

You can do this on your own, but in my experience you'll get much better value when you work with a buddy.

Agree on 100% confidentiality

If you work with a buddy you must agree that the conversation is confidential. Agree that total non-disclosure applies. This means is you are able to openly discuss your business and it goes no further.

Agree on idea ownership

If you work with someone else, agree that everything that comes out of the conversation remains your *Intellectual Property* (IP). If it's your strategy, you own whatever insights and ideas come out the session – *100*% - even if the other person contributed.

I have conducted hundreds of strategy sessions that resulted in my clients making a lot of money. But that's how this works. Discuss this with your buddy ahead of time. Get that agreement up front or don't use them for this activity. If there's any doubt, choose someone else.

I don't want your buddy claiming they gave you a million dollar idea and now want a percentage. They agree to help no strings attached.

Don't over complicate it

The questions are pretty straightforward so just work with each question *as you understand it*. Of course, you'll need to add more detail if you progress through to a formal business plan but for now, you just want a snapshot.

Aim to complete all the questions and the strategy in one sitting. 90 minutes is about right.

If you don't know, say, 'I don't know.'

Saying, *'I don't know'* is actually a good answer. Most people don't have all the answers (especially to the finance questions). But then, note the gap in your answers and make it a priority to get those answers.

After the workshop

First, answer all ten questions and record your answers. Then, at a separate time, listen back to the recordings and make notes.

I've found that if you get an ring binder and coloured divider tabs – one for each question – you end up with a very useful sectioned working document. People who do it this way tend to get far superior results.

Just the questions only

Parts 4 and *5* might seem similar because in both parts I ask the question and give working examples. If you want the questions only without any explanation, case studies or notes jump straight to the *Appendix*. A selection of suitable topic-related questions are listed there.

So, if you are ready, let's begin with …

STARTING!

Question 1
Why exactly did you start your business?

This is the most important question of all.

Why exactly did you want to start your own business?

Take your time. Whatever comes to mind. To be my own boss, freedom, self-determination, more money and so on.

It might surprise you that most people do not answer this question easily or in any detail. So really deep dive into that question. There's gold to be found there but you might have to dig to find the nuggets.

For best results try and say *more* about things. Elaborate on your answers no matter how irrelevant it seems. A business is incredibly rewarding but it will also demand a lot from you so you'd better be clear why you are signing on for business ownership and everything that demands of you.

Your answers will fall into three obvious categories: *practical, clinical* and *contribution*.

You obviously want *practical* outcomes - for example you want your financial needs to be met.

But you also want your *clinical* needs met such as the need to do satisfying and meaningful work. And most people I find ultimately want to make a difference in the lives of others, to *contribute* or give back.

You have already racked up so much value in your qualifications, skills, experience, knowledge, accreditations, life lessons, methods, tips, tools and resources you have gathered over your career or your lifetime. One big reason to start a business is to leverage that value.

Your business should deliver lifestyle benefits. So, what key lifestyle benefits do you imagine your business will deliver?

Don't just say *'a better lifestyle.'* Be very specific. Drill into what *'a better lifestyle'* means to you. Paint a much clearer picture. In our session I'd get you to elaborate because you need to have a clear yardstick for measuring success.

Once you know what your business is intended to deliver you can check the results. Is your business giving you more family time? Are you able to go snowboarding twice a year? Do you have nicer home? Or more money? How much money? Are you happier? More satisfied? Healthier? Less stressed?"

Your business will demand a lot from you so your *big why* must be big enough to inspire your on-going commitment.

How do you want to impact the world? What are you helping your target customers to do, have and become?

Neil started his own engineering business specialising in fire safety devices fitted to mining vehicles. I'm talking about those really big ones with wheels the size of a house. Neil knows there's a probability of a fire because of harsh operating and harsh conditions. If you are the driver you want that fire to be detected, suppressed or better still, extinguished as soon as possible. So Neil's business saves lives.

You might also answer the question:

Why do I do what I do?

David is a fuel consultant and Nigel is a debt reduction expert. Both of them have worked in industries where there is massive waste of money. And both want their clients to soften their carbon footprint.

Anne, a trained nurse, trains supermarket staff how to respond to a cardiac arrest and use a defibrillator. As more of the *Baby Boomers* turn 70, cardiac arrest is on the rise. And you are statistically more likely to have a cardiac arrest while food shopping!

She supplies defibrillators and training. Why? Because her husband had a cardiac arrest and could have been saved had one been available.

You might focus on deeply held beliefs or values that will shape and underpin your business.

There is a lot of material available on core values and needs. Tony Robbins adapted six needs, there's Maslow's *Hierarchy of Needs,* Dr Steven Stosny's *Core Values* and John Bligh's *Core Beliefs.*

My values are around growth and contribution and family. *BNO!,* ironically a lifestyle publication, was stressful and did not deliver a pleasant lifestyle.

Whatever system you choose, at the very basic level you want your business to meet your needs and align with your core values.

Your turn

So why do you want to start your own business? (Or if you are already established, why *did* you start your own business originally?) Once again, what insights did you get from this section and what are some clear next steps for you?

STARTING!

Four Key Reasons You Start a Business

This might help. There are four key reasons why most savvy people start a business. None is better than the other and each carries different implications.

"I want a nice lifestyle."

The first reason for starting a business is to have a nice lifestyle. Simple. Great reason.

Nice house, nice stuff, nice car, holidays, weekends with family, sport, travel, theatre tickets, restaurants, BBQs with mates, nice schools, pony club, gadgets, toys, hobbies etc. (Technically, you need annual revenues of about $600k-$4M to qualify as a *lifestyle* business.)

Once you achieve a nice lifestyle the goal is to maintain it. You business has to sustain that result.

I wanted *BNO!* to give me a lifestyle for my family. However it did not deliver anything that remotely resembled lifestyle benefits. I got clear on what my benefits my business should deliver and now, I do have a lifestyle business that actually delivers lifestyle outcomes.

A *lifestyle business* has a *shorter-term focus* and is all about how you *feel*. You typically think about right now or in 90-day time frames. You tend to watch the top and bottom line as it relates to maintaining your lifestyle.

"I want to leave a legacy. I want to make a difference."

A *legacy business* is still about how it feels but is has a *longer-term* focus. Think about a grandfather-to-father-and-son family business spanning several generations.

My dad started a travel agency. He wanted to put *Priestley and Son* on the signs. He aspired to an intergenerational family business. Sadly, I didn't want to be a travel agent.

Parents these days can no longer assume that children will want to carry on the family business, as in previous generations. Young people have their own ideas about their vocations in a rapidly changing world, constantly offering opportunities in new industries.

Legacy was once a valid business model but today tax laws don't seem to encourage longevity. UK *Inheritance Tax* laws, as an example, make intergenerational businesses almost untenable, unless you know accountants and lawyers who can set up Family Trusts to protect family holdings like property. The successful business exists to fund a property portfolio - the real legacy.

The other form of legacy is having a social enterprise component to the business. For example, you might bequest a percentage of your profits to charity. So you see the business as means of creating a legacy - for others.

"I want a fast exit."

This approach can be *short-term* and set up purely with *money* or an exit valuation in mind. In other words you start it with the express goal of a trade sale, a merger and acquisition (M&A) or a management buy out (MBO).

If I had been smart, I should have set up *BNO!* to become so annoying to my competitors that they bought my little newspaper and simply paid me to disappear. I didn't know this strategy at the time.

Exit is a legitimate business model that is used a lot more than you think. People buy and flip businesses.

If you watch *The Apprentice* (UK), Lord Sugar usually wants an exit valuation within 3-5 years. He wants the apprentice to buy out his option.

The key to this approach is: you start the business to sell it. It has a relatively short term focus.

I believe *One Direction*, the most successful music act in history, a global boy-band music sensation, was a five-year proposition. It was never intended as a long-term entity. And it appears it achieved the intended financial outcome.

"I want recurring profits."

This business model is still about *money* but is a *longer-term* proposition set up to extract recurring profits and dividends from the business.

John created engineering software and sold licenses to distributors for his products, which earn recurring revenues. He does very little with this project but it ticks along quietly earning him income.

A rock band is a recurring profits model because the aim is to earn royalties over many years. The *Gerry Rafferty Family Trust* reportedly still earns £80,000 a year from *Baker Street,* one of Gerry's chart-topping hits.

Lifestyle and *Legacy* business are all about feelings and emotions and *Exit* and *Recurring Profits* are all about money - but obviously you can get a blend.]

Money earned from John's engineering licenses give him a great lifestyle.

Which one sounds like you?

Of course, each of these business drivers require different ways of running the business.

Your turn

For now, reflect on what you've read and add any insights to *Question 1*. Get clear answers to the following questions:

- Why did I start my business?
- What benefits do I want my business to deliver?
- What is the key style of my business - *lifestyle, legacy, exit* or *recurring profit?*

The assumption test

The big assumption here is you will be a lot better off starting and running your own business. The litmus test is you are perfectly clear on why you are opting for business ownership.

Question 2
What exactly is your business concept?

Often I find that people cannot clearly explain the idea for their business. This question will help you explain your business concept more clearly.

What exactly is your business concept?

Remember, you are recording this so talk as long as you feel you need to. Describe the idea for your business. Take as long as you want but try and be as clear as you can.

It helps to include a little about your background. You may want to mention your qualifications and maybe key aspects from your career or work history. You may want to talk a little about the career journey you've been on so far, and how you came up with the idea for your business.

Whenever I talk to business owners about how they got started I am always fascinated by their journey.

Tania is an engineer but now works as a therapist. What's fascinating is how she went from engineering to therapy. If you've pivoted in your career, you need to describe that.

Louise started out as a fashion designer and is now a specialist in designing customer experiences for major High Street retailers.

I started out a teacher, became a publisher, then a marketer, then a business coach and trainer.

Even if you've been in the *same* industry you've still been on a journey. Ivan started out a marine biologist and ended up in project management within the same sector.

Henry is a financial planner and he had a dazzling business until *Black Friday* in August 1987. Then his whole world got thrown upside down.

Over the next three years he questioned his business and his industry and after doing a value-based financial advisory course he switched from focusing on financial products to designing life plans. Now he makes *money fit your life* rather than your *life revolving around money*.

Kev and Phil, also financial planners, started their careers working for a company having to sell a set range of house branded products to clients that often were not the best fit. They went on to create their own independent financial advisory business that specialises in helping business owners achieve a genuine, sustainable lifestyle income and lifestyle using best-fit solutions.

Henry, Kev and Phil arrived at similar conclusions but offer totally different and equally effective client solutions.

Everyone has an interesting story. So talk about your background and the journey you've been on.

Invariably your idea will combine several components.

April wants to start a sales training business. She has had over 19 years experience in sales training in blue chip companies. Currently a sales trainer with *IBM*, she wants to start her own independent sales training consultancy that will include *individual* and *team coaching, intensive training* and *full day workshops*.

So it seems her sales consultancy idea has already got three or four product possibilities.

Your answers might overlap with *Question 1*, but that's OK. Why do you want to start this business? How did you come up with this business idea? Why do you do what you do?

There is one other question worth exploring that relates to *Question 7*.

Why do you think your idea will work?

Quite often the idea you have, or something very similar, has been done by someone else, somewhere else.

That's how *BNO!* got started.

So your idea therefore might have an existing track record. If so, do lots of research and be clear about why your take on the idea will be better or different to what providers already offer in this sector. An investor is looking for that point of difference and proof of concept if they intend to go ahead and invest.

You can get that data from existing industry research. Or you might run several small side projects to determine if there is enough uptake for the idea.

As an example, business often commences as a series of one-off promotional campaigns. Perhaps you have racked up enough success and sufficient sales data to suggest that a sustainable business exists.

As a rule once you have explored this first question, stop the recording, save it and start a new recording for the next question.

The assumption test

The big assumption here is you can explain your idea clearly and others will get it, care about it and want to pay for it in sufficient numbers that suggest its sustainable.

Your turn

OK, what insights did you get from this section and what are some key actions steps?

STARTING!

Question 3:
Who exactly is this for?

This is such an important question to explore.

**"Who is you main target customer? Why them?
What problem/s have these people got
that needs your solution?"**

I am constantly staggered at how new and even established business owners are unclear about who their target customer is, their key problems or the explicit problem their product or service will solve for that specific customer.

It's usually a combination of four issues:

- It's not clear who your target market is and who it is for, exactly
- It's not clear the problem that you're trying to solve for them
- The value proposition (result or promise) isn't clear
- Your positioning is unclear.

So let's explore these four elements.

Your target market

Ask questions such as:

- Who is this for, exactly?
- Who are your target customers?
- Who is your ideal preferred customer?
- Who is your product best suited to?
- Who would you prefer to work with?
- Who can afford you?

Try not to say that your products and services are for *people* or *everyone*. Your business is not for *people* or *everyone*. For starters, not *everyone* may be able to afford you.

The big mistake I see over and over again is trying to be all things to everyone. If I had a tool of choice for most businesses I'd say identify a specific target market, niche or micro-niche even.

Your ideal target customer should match five criteria:

- You like them
- You can get a great result for them
- They can afford you
- They can afford to implement your recommendations
- They'll refer business to you

Your ideal target client's avatar

One way to get highly specific about just who your target custom is to design an ideal target customer *avatar* - a detailed composite description.

Maybe you work with professional women aged 35-50, or you work with mid-tier companies with up to a 100 employees, or with companies with turnovers greater than $5M.

My target market is ambitious owner managers of SMEs running established companies with turnovers between £300k and £7M who want to grow, scale or exit their business.

Or maybe your target market has a specific professional problem such as ineffective teams, absenteeism, poor productivity, bullying or poor sales or high-end problems such as innovation or sustainability issues.

You might be looking for clients based on the amount of time you work with them (minimum 3 months) or the minimum amount of money they need to spend with you (say $25,000).

Your target market is usually based on reliable research, informed industry experience or even a formal client analysis.

As an example, Kevin is an accountant who *only* works with family-run service businesses averaging $250,000 in revenues. He really likes them, he can consistently get a great result for that niche, they can afford him, and they can afford to implement his suggestions. And because they get results they are happy to refer.

When he did a client analysis of his total customer base he discovered 16% were husband and wife family-run businesses in trades such as plumbing, electrical, building, painting etc. These little businesses had revenues of USD$250k pa, they usually had 1-5 employees, the business was capital intense and they usually had refinancing and tax headaches.

It was only 16% but that 16% generates 67% of his overall revenues.

Dr Rene is a doctor in Chinese Medicine who used to treat everyone for anything. She now *only* treats very busy, time-poor executive women suffering from hand, neck and facial psoriasis.

Her target client can afford the 12-18 months treatment required to get that condition under control. Dr Rene suffered psoriasis herself for many years prior to qualifying as a doctor and on average spent $10,000 a year on topical treatments that didn't resolve the cause.

She developed a comprehensive approach that treats psoriasis from the inside out with a focus on improving gut health and nutrient absorption. Of course, she also focuses on diet, stress and maintaining ideal dermatology.

If you say your target market is for *people* or *everyone,* unless your business model is geared for mass marketing, give your target customer a lot more careful thought.

Problem

What problem are you trying to solve for your target market?

- Dr Rene treats psoriasis.
- Kevin fixes cash flow problems.

Here's an interesting twist to the question.

What are your target customers trying to get done?

Usually your clients are after a specific result.

- Dr Rene's customers are trying to have clear skin and be free of the irritating and embarrassing skin condition called psoriasis.
- Kevin's clients are trying to get their revenues from $250k up to $500k pa.
- Tommy is a fitness trainer. His clients are mainly women and they are trying to drop two dress sizes for summer or for some special event like a wedding.
- Daryl's clients are trying to buy exquisite, one-off, hand crafted pieces of high-end furniture.
- Dominique's corporate clients want to have high performing and ethical staff.

Three Dominant Problems

Your customer may be experiencing lot of problems so first get a long list of all those problems and then distill the list down to just three dominant problems that prevent them from having the results they want.

George is a cabinetmaker and he specialises in doing refurbishments for medical centres. His clients usually have a ten-year lease on their current premises and if they are going to relocate or refurbish they need to start thinking about it about two years out before the lease expires. Under a year and they have pretty much missed the window of opportunity to do either and end up signing another ten year lease on a property that may no longer meet their needs.

We listed the problems that his clients experience and got to about 168 problems. Those problems distilled down to about 11 key themes from which George identified the top three problems - pain points - that most-resonate with his clients.

They were:

1. No idea of the process
2. No idea of how much time it would take; and
3. No idea of the cost.

The ultimate problem of course is running out of time and re-signing a lease on premises that is not fit-for-purpose! George helps his clients avoid that massive problem.

Here are some more examples.

- Tommy identified the top three key things stopping his clients from dropping two dress sizes. Tommy has solutions for those three problems.
- Dr Rene identified the top three key things that prevent her clients' skin from being psoriasis free. And Dr Rene's treatment addresses those three issues.
- And Kevin identified the top three major problems that seem to consistently inhibit his clients from hitting $500K in revenues. And he definitely has a solution to address those issues.

So a good question to explore is:

What three dominant problems are stopping your clients from getting the result they want most?

Your Promise

What is the promise your product or service makes? What's the outcome or result your customer will get? What outcome do you want for your target customer?

Since childhood we have understood the concept of a promise, when our parents said: *'If you are good, I promise you will get an ice-cream.'* Or, *'If you are good, I promise you will get a new bike for Christmas.'* Your value proposition is just like a promise.

- If you work with Kevin, the accountant, the typical result is you will hit revenues of $500k per annum.
- If you are a patient of Dr Rene, the skin specialist, the typical result is your skin will clear up.
- If you train with Tommy, the fitness trainer, typically you drop two dress sizes.
- If you hire April, the sales trainer, typically you get a dramatic uplift in sales performance and revenues.
- If you hire Dominique, the corporate lawyer, you will find out if you have a self-serving culture of bullying and address that issue. Or you will discover if your business has slavery somewhere in your supply chain and resolve that ethical issue!
- If you are a patient of Dr Leo, the dentist, you will get a nice smile.
- If you work with George you will either refurbish or relocate your medical practice before your ten-year lease expires.

What do you promise?

You may have answers for these questions but I usually find that this area needs more formal and informal research. A lot of business people do not have clear answers in this area but they start the business anyway!

Understand if you have vague answers for the questions in the section you will be leaving money on the table or worse you will be losing money.

Your Positioning

Get out some paper and draw a cross. Label one axis *premium* or *budget*; and label the other axis *product* or *relationships*.

So you are either a *premium* or *budget* priced business and the emphasis is on either *products* or *relationships*.

A *premium relationship* business might be the guru model of Tony Robbins. A *premium product* might be *KPMG, PWC* or *Goldman Sachs*. The clue is whether you know the owner of the business. Does it have a face? If your business is faceless it's probably a product business right now.

A *budget product* might be anyone who is cheap and cheerful. A *budget relationship* is advice Uncle George will give you over a beer.

You can be profitable at *any* of those positions provided you are clear on how you take profits at that position.

A *premium product* is all about what your customer *gets* – amazing products, processes or proprietary services and a premium relationship is about what your customer *feels* from highly engaging customer relationships and a remarkable customer experience.

So do you provide a *premium product* or a *premium relationship*, a *budget product* or a *budget relationship*?

But you can only be one; not all. You have to choose just one position.

Dominique has a small consulting business that does organisational and cultural change in companies helping management and employees reach their full potential. Her business is about *people* so she needs to position her business as a *premium relationship*.

But her website screams *budget product*! Be careful how you position or intend to position yourself, knowing you must follow through with consistency in your branding.

I urge you to read *Positioning* by Jack Trout. The case studies are a little old but the principles are still incredibly relevant to your business.

Trout confirms that you need to be crystal clear about your target customer, too.

Once again, I get clients to create an avatar of their ideal client that includes *demographic i*nformation (age, gender, income etc.) and *psychographic* information (why they buy). You need to know this information.

It is worth repeating: you cannot be all things to everyone and the way forward is *niching*. To put that into context here's a little history lesson.

Positioning 101
When I started in marketing and advertising the best way of promoting anything was mass media: newspapers, magazines, direct mail, TV and radio. But to gain any significant result you needed deep pockets to buy newspaper and magazine ad space; or TV or radio airtime.

Above line marketing was all about *transactions* - what I could sell - and the methods were tried and tested press-based methods such as A/B split testing and page placement or prime time loadings.

In 1984, I remember a mate calling me, all excited, saying: "Andrew, you have to come over and look at this!" He had just bought the new *Apple Macintosh* with *Pagemaker* software and I instantly realised everything was about to change.

By 1995, dial-up internet was gaining momentum along with the now defunct modem connection screech. The internet was treated as the new mass medium marketing *transaction* tool.

By 1998, the rush was well and truly on to have the biggest and best website but it was still essentially the offline transaction world of mass marketing taken online. Websites were expensive to create and maintain so once again, you needed deep pockets.

My first insight about the web, social networks and niching was the chat rooms - notorious for dating chat rooms. That's where I first heard the term *niche.*

I can remember joining a niche chat room for marketers. The conversation was brilliant, but it was still all about transacting.

The internet started to change with *WordPress* in 2003 with blog sites, basically cheap DIY landing pages. Suddenly, you could create your website quickly, for free. I believe blogs broke the stranglehold the press had over information. Instead of one newspaper suddenly there were millions of small 'news' disseminators and opinion pieces. Suddenly everyone had an opinion on everything.

I believe the world really changed when *Facebook* came along. *Facebook*, launched on February 4, 2004 by Mark Zuckerberg, was originally intended as a social networking site was for *Harvard* students only and therefore a niche.

Facebook was excellent for creating flashmob social events, parties and meetings just for *Harvard* people.

Then it became micro-niches targeting closed invitation-only communities just for computing geeks, law students, business and psychology majors and so on. Basically, it was about *relationships*. Importantly, anyone trying to *transact* was asked to leave or ejected from the group.

In 2005, *YouTube* was launched and suddenly the strangle hold major network TV had on broadcast video was broken. Instead of three or four networks controlling what you watched, who you watched, when they wanted you to watch it, and where and how you watched (on TV screens only), suddenly there were millions of small channels to get information and entertainment from for free on your computer screens. And anyone could create a channel and build and audience.

Now mobile devices such as smart phones and tablets allow us to view shows wherever we are: on a train or bus, in the park or café!

Prior to 2003, it cost an exorbitant amount of money to disseminate information. Suddenly, we all had a global reach for free or low cost. Before the internet, it simply wasn't viable to market to a small niche. The web made it possible to target and reach highly specialised even obscure niches easily and profitably.

E-commerce has been around for over 40 years with electronic data interchange (EDI) from 1960 onwards, but secure online payments quadrupled between 2011 and 2014. So a highly niched fishing gear manufacturer could now sell Spanish mackerel rods and reels worldwide profitably.

The key to success is *valued relationships*.

The fishing gear business is run by fishermen who only fish for Spanish mackerel. Their *YouTube* videos, podcasts and blogs are all about Spanish mackerel.

You cannot fake competence as a Spanish mackerel fisherman, in the same way you could not fake being a *Harvard* student. The tribe knows what's *real* and what's not and because it is real they trust and engage with that e-tailer. But the relationship comes first and the transaction *might* come second, not the other way round.

The old way is *'Buy something and I'll be your friend',* now it's *'Be my friend and I might buy something from you'.*

But your tribe refer and a happy tribe become your relational marketing department.

Big trends like social media take at least 20 years or more before we understand them and we are just over ten years into *Facebook* so we are still in relatively early days.

The reason people are now steering away from a platform like *Facebook* is because it seems to have veered away from it's *relational* roots. It's becoming a *disruptive transaction* site with automatically playing video content and paid content.

I understand the need for *Facebook* to monetise its website given that within five years over 400 million people were using it. But more and more people are expressing concerns about the commercial information *Facebook* gleans about you and the algorithms *Facebook* has developed to pester you with ads.

We expect it of *Amazon* - if you bought this you will like this. *Amazon* learns your preferences but it's a transaction site, so we accept that. But *Facebook* is a relationship site. There's a big lesson right there if you want to make niche marketing work.

People are now steering away from *Twitter*, originally a social network, which is now like viewing a continuous 24-hour long tsunami of commercials.

I believe the online world has well and truly entered this relational phase but we are still trying to *transact* on *relational* social networks.

Relational marketing is about valued relationships. Real relationships.

I have a client who is a specialist in interim management. He has gone back to a closed invitation-only group where the people inside that group have a common interest and speak a common language and the platform owner cannot use the participants' data or have the ability to drop promotional content into the middle of a conversation. Ironically, that group is worth a fortune in business to my client because the glue of that niche is trusted relationships.

It all starts by identifying who exactly you want to do business with and in *Question 5* you start to explore relevant and appropriate routes to market that engage that niche in meaningful ways.

Your turn

OK, what key insights did you get from this section and what are some obvious actions steps? Can you identify who exactly is your ideal, target customer? Who would you love as a customer?

The assumption test

The big assumption here is you have identified the right target market and you have access to them. There is no point designing a business for billionaires if you haven't got a route to market.

The other assumption is you have correctly identified their problem set and confirmed that it resonates.

I gave several case studies where clients did a lot of desk searching and surveying to confirm there was a minimum viable market willing to pay for products and services designed to meet their needs. The assumption is they *want* what you are selling, not just you think they need it.

Question 4
Who is on your operating team?

Whatever you are trying to get done will probably require the input of others. The questions to ask yourself here are:

- Who's on your operating team?
- Who do you need on your operating team?
- Who is on the internal team (employees/partners) and your extended external (suppliers/sub-contractors/flexible teams)?
- Are you adequately resourced or under-resourced?

Here's a story to help you understand the importance of these questions.

Warren worked for one of the large shipping companies but was made redundant in 2009 because of staff cutbacks. His expertise is in checking the hulls of huge container ships for problems like rust perforations.

He decided to buy a specialist scanner for $75,000 and subcontract his services to his previous employer. His first job came quickly. It was to scan the hulls of three container boats.

Fantastic, right? Wrong. Firstly, he only had one machine. And secondly, he lacked the available manpower to survey one boat on his own, let alone three. It was like he won the Lottery and then had to return all the money.

His oversight was immediately obvious. Warren had set up a one-man business to do the work that requires several machines and a team of experts.

Here's another example.

If you own a fleet of fifty or more trucks Daryl can save you a significant amount of money on your fuel bills.

Daryl's clients operate lorry fleets that deliver the length and breadth of both the UK and Europe. His clients usually spend £45,000 a month on fuel.

Daryl's clients are located in key regional centres throughout the UK; and there is a shortage of local driver trainers and fuel consultants in those areas. Daryl has subcontractors but the day rates, travel allowance and accommodation costs strip most of the profit out of any contracts.

Brian and Shireene started an App development company and worked 16-hour days to fulfill projects that require a team of at least eight coders.

And of course, I set up a newspaper with two people that needed a much bigger team!

In all these examples the common theme is being under resourced and over-stretched.

Who is on your operating team? Who do you need?

Your operating team is comprised of *internal* and *external* people.

Your *internal team* are usually paid employees but can include part-time and casual staff. Your *external team* includes subcontractors.

But this can also include service providers such as your accountant, bookkeeper; and suppliers such as power and water, internet provider, couriers, the postal service, insurers – basically *anyone* in the background essential to keeping your business operating.

Remember the four parts of the business?

That includes marketing and sales, management and administration, operations and finance.

People are needed in those four main areas. Right now, you might do all of those jobs yourself or you might be slowly employing, delegating or outsourcing those roles.

I get my coaching clients to complete an organisational and functions chart and assign names to each function.

Investors look at the three 'M's - *management, management* and *management.* If they are going to invest in your business they want to be totally reassured that you have adequate human resources to get them a return on their investment.

It is a very dumb mistake to start a business that needs a team and you don't have a team. I learned this crucial lesson the hard way. I did everything on my own and it nearly killed me! I closed that business down after six months and was left exhausted and with a debt of $25,000 which took nearly five years to pay off.

Your turn

So, talk about who is on your operating team. And who you need.

The assumption test

The big assumption here is you have the resources and capacity to deliver a full and remarkable result. Or that you can do everything on your own and punch well above your weight. The other assumption is your business will generate the revenues to afford a team of full time, part time, casuals, sub contractors and suppliers.

Carefully check for any other assumptions like these.

STARTING!

Question 5:
What is the route to market?

These questions focus on your route to a minimum viable market.

- Who is your target market?
- What is the proof that a market exists?
- What is the route-to-market?
- What is your sales process? How will you sell to them?
- And who are your competitors?

Your Target Market

We covered this in detail in *Question 3* but its worth revisiting. Who is your main customer? Your ideal preferred target market? Your target market is typically described in terms of *demographics* (quantifiable attributes such as age, gender, income, size of market, geography etc); and *psychographics* (qualitative attributes such as why they buy).

Hard data can be gleaned from a number of sources such as your national office of statistics right through to your own client analysis research. Soft data usually comes from surveys, interviews and anecdotes.

Donald started a coaching business knowing that he had access to 4.5 million small businesses nationally. He narrowed that search down to businesses with annual revenues greater than $250,000.

In addition to government data, he personally interviewed over 700 small businesses to ensure their were enough expressions of interest in his offering and pricing to justify commencing the business.

Proof that a minimum viable market exists

How have you proven a minimum viable market exists?

Donald surveyed over 700 small business owners to identify what they wanted and how much they were willing to pay for his coaching services.

Some business owners I talk to have done some superficial research but most and done zero research. All they have is an idea and a suspicion that there might be a need for what they are offering.

Warren knew that shipping companies needed safety checks performed on the hulls of their boats and was delighted when he won his first contract. But he did not research expectations about delivery requirements and turnaround times.

Warren and his team are expected to travel to wherever a ship is berthed and start straight away.

Warren could not economically assemble a flexible delivery team, *and* provide, travel, accommodation, meals *and* transfers as well as hire extra equipment - all costs Warren failed to factor into the costing of his proposal.

Warren quickly realised that his business idea was not viable.

I worked with a sales trainer who accepted a contract to train a team of 60 salespeople. The company accepted his proposal but failed to mention that the teams were located in four different geographical locations. The travel, day rates and accommodation killed the profit in that project.

Earlier we met Alex. If you recall he was going to borrow a big chunk of money to purchase a container load of old model cell phones sitting in a holding yard in Heathrow London, UK and ship them to a country in Africa.

Alex finally did some research and discovered that the phones had to be capable of receiving downloadable digital content such as agriculture reports. Mobile infrastructure in this African country was pretty good and the government was even offering grants to develop content for remote rural agribusinesses.

Alex discovered that while the consignment of handsets had a retail value of $400,000 the recurring revenues from downloadable content was about $217m annually.

Alex decided to learn more about the grants process. Subsequently, Alex pivoted and abandoned the plan to buy and sell superceded handsets.

He now helps App developers successfully apply for content development grants - a viable and profitable business.

That is the power of good research. It could have gone pear shaped. He might have borrowed money for handsets that could not receive downloadable content!

Your Route-to-Market

Do you have a marketing strategy? How are you going to market your offering? A good question is: how do you get intend to get your customers? The route to market is the most efficient means of marketing that finds and reaches your target customers that gets them into your sales funnel.

Will you attract customers through newspaper advertising, social media, events, word of mouth, cold calling, footfall traffic, a web site and SEO strategies? What marketing channels do you think you should use and why? And, at what cost? And how will you know it's working?

Dr Rene regularly blogs and uploads videos to *YouTube*. She blogs and writes articles on *LinkedIn* and then *Tweets* the links. She also embeds links in direct emails. She does a great deal of public speaking and offers potential clients free reports and white papers. Of course she gets a lot of word-of-mouth client referrals.

Sales process

If you find a customer how are you going to sell to them? What is your step-by-step sales process?

Bernie's sales process starts with cold calling target prospects. This leads to an informal 20-minute chat and if appropriate he suggests a half-day strategy session that determines one of three levels of consulting packages.

I once worked with a global engineering firm. Their sales process is very complicated and highly regulated. You can't directly pitch and close a client. You have to go through protracted tendering and procurement process. But they know that process and how it works.

Whatever your business or industry there will be a sales process to suit.

Dr Rene ask a client to book an appointment for an obligation-free chat. This leads to an initial consultation with recommendations, risks and options. She will recommend one of three possible treatment paths that suits the patient's specific needs (mild, moderate and serious). The client then officially commences the relevant treatment plan.

In my coaching business, I start the process with a free or low cost information product, clients book a two-hour business strategy session and some go through to a full coaching programme.

How will your sales process work?

Competitors

You need to think about your direct competitors. Do some desk research especially if you are entering an already existing marketplace.

Neil is an employment lawyer and he did a *Google* search on *Employment Law London*. His search revealed over 120 competitors. He methodically went through each law firm and examined their service offerings.

He discovered that most legal websites are a confused jumble of services and legal jargon.

He generated a table of services and was able to identify a gap in the market: *reputation damage*. Apparently, if and executive is involved in an employment dispute and it goes to court, whatever the outcome the ruling will appear in court reports and the media. This can make it impossible for an executive to get another job especially if it was acrimonious. The ability to contain reputation damage through smart PR made him stand out in a very crowded market.

Remember Donald who sells business coaching? And Kevin who is an accountant?

Both decided to focus on family-run small businesses. Donald provides business development services and Kevin provides tax efficient strategies but both can offer services not provided by competitors, well or at all, that their target market can afford. Importantly, services they can deliver profitably.

Both offerings were based on research not guesswork and conjecture.

Too many entrepreneurs have done next to no analysis or competitor research whatsoever and then wonder why there are no customers and why they cannot make a profitable business out of their ideas.

These questions urge you to explore how you intend to reach and sell products and services to your target customers.

Your turn

What are your insights? Does a minimum viable business target exist for your offering; and what is the route to that market?

The assumption test

The obvious assumption here is you can access your target customer; and your marketing will work. The big assumption is that you are differentiated and unique enough to have cut-through. You might be entering a crowded, noisy market space but your marketing will cut through that noise and be meaningful to your customers.

STARTING!

Question 6:
What do you sell?
And how much do you charge?

Every business has a core offering - the product that makes you the most money. Ideally, you have an on-ramp of related free or lower cost products that logically leads your target customers to that core offering. Or you need one.

We call that your *product ecosystem*.

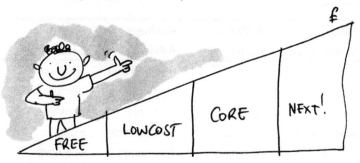

This chapter will help you develop your product ecosystem.

- What do you sell?
- What are the price points?
- What is the cheapest thing you sell?
- What is the most expensive thing you sell?
- Is there a free or low cost entry point to your core offering?

For example my product ecosystem includes:

Free/No Cost	Low Cost <£1000	Core Offering
My website	Business Leadership	Coaching
Free downloads	Profile	
My blog		Option 1
YouTube videos	90-minute business	Option 2
Podcasts	strategy	Option 3
Free Reports		
Workshops	1/2 day strategy day	Retainers
Advice clinics	Full day strategy day	

Some businesses have products that fall into logical product, price or complexity bandwidths. Most accountants offer around 140 accounting services that can be organised into *compliance, business support, business advisory* and *wealth services*. The core offering in this case is *business advisory* services.

Basic Compliance	Business Support	Business Advisory	Wealth Services
Individual tax	NIC	Business plans	Succession
returns	VAT	Management	plans
Self	PAYE	accounts	Pensions
assessments	Corp tax	Tax planning	Estate
	EOY filing	Tax rulings	planning
	Quickbooks	Pension funds	CGT
	training		Inheritance

A smart home technology business had a complex range of services and focused on the actual brand name appliances that they would supply. This made quoting a protracted and costly exercise that could stretch out over weeks and months.

The product ecosystem works because it's logical, easier to create and it takes your client on a journey they understand.

Free/No Cost	Low Cost <£1000	Core Offering
Website	In-home	Lighting >£10k
Downloads	consultation with	Audio >£50k
Brochure	builder, interior	Cinema > £100k
Social media	designer or architect	Climate > £150k
YouTube videos	Heritage listed	Security > £200
Checklists	property checks	
Free Reports	Architect services	Packages > £250k
Smart Home		
discovery session		

A kitchen designer created the following product ecosystem.

Free/No Cost	Low Cost <£1000	Core Offering
Website	Kitchen design	£5-10k
Downloads - reports	service	£10-15k
YouTube videos	Appliance scheme	£15-20k
Social media	Interior design	£20-50K
Company brochure	service	£50K+
Product brochures		
Measure and quote		

Their core offering was segmented into *ballpark* price and inclusion bandwidths that made quoting incredibly easy. Clients could see what they would get for their budget. An immediate benefit was customers stopped asking for or expecting to get full remodelling service on a tight budget.

£5-10k	£10-15k	£15-20k	£20-25k	£25k+
Bench tops,	New	Cabinetry,	Structural	Full kitchen
cupboard	cabinets	install and	and smart	extensions
doors,	Tops, doors	fit-out	technology	Fit out
fascias and	and fascias	Appliances		Appliance
decorating	Appliances			etc

Remember April, the sales training consultant? Her product ecosystem includes:

Free/No Cost	Low Cost <£1000	Core Offering
Website	Book	1-2-1 Coaching for
Downloads	CD set	sales managers
Social media	Online e-course	Team coaching
YouTube videos		On going training
Webinars	Sales skills profiling	
Reports	Lunch'n'learn	
Brochure	training sessions	
Free opt-in PDF	Workshops (1/2 day,	
course	full day, 2 day)	

One obvious conclusion is that you need to identify the elements that will be included in each section of your product ecosystem. Start with the basics.

- Have you got a website?
- Are you using social media platforms to drive traffic?
- Do you have online videos? A blog?
- Downloadable information sheets?
- A sales brochure?

Importantly, your product ecosystem must take your client on a journey that makes sense.

Like the kitchen company it's a good idea to think about what a client gets with each element in your product ecosystem.

I worked with an accounting firm who offered clients 143 services! We organised those services into logical categories:

- Compliance
- Business support
- Business advisory
- Wealth creation

We then created a *Schedule of Services* for every item:

Item	What you get Inclusions	Real Value to the client	Price
Individual Tax Return	Collate the tax return information. Complete the forms. Electronically submit the forms to HMRC. Provide proof of filing to the client.	The client has a convenient, accurate, one-stop, end of year service that is easy to complete. Filing is done on their behalf to meet the deadline There are no penalty fees.	£90 plus VAT

You've probably guessed the *Real Value to the Client* is the most important column in the schedule because it describes the value the client really gets for their money.

Even though it took several months to complete, the accounting team gained so much insight from this activity.

It became apparent that 80% of their services made them next to no income at all and yet they had included those services *just in case*. They were in fact trying to be all things to everyone. After much discussion they decided to niche down their service offerings and focus on companies turning over £300,000 minimum.

Eventually 64% of their client book - all the individual tax return clients - were sold off to another accounting firm.

Incredibly, the business grew because they could now focus on their £300,000 plus companies who needed more business advisory services.

I have helped several accounting practices niche down. One firm now only works with the creative industries while another only works with wealthy families with £25m+ in assets.

This strategy also works for products. Peter has over 3,500 stock items that segment into 13 categories.

Peter identified that 23% of his stock generated 73% of his revenues; and 40% of stock only generated about 3% of revenues. He ditched underperforming stock items with no loss of business.

Of course the assumption is you can sell. Your customer goes on a sales journey too. A typical sales journey might include your marketing, an inbound enquiry or an outbound sales call, an appointment, a presentation, a proposal and a sale.

It's important to know how many leads are generated by your marketing, how many calls per appointment, how many appointments per proposal and how many proposal per sale.

You need to know your numbers.

Can you see how the information here might have a direct relationship to the previous route-to-market question? The questions work in isolation but they are inter-connected too.

Your turn

What insights did you get from this section? What exactly do you sell starting with the lowest cost item right through to your most expensive? What are the obvious product or service categories in your business? What are the most and least profitable? What could you include for free or low cost that will guide your client towards your core offering?

The assumption test

The obvious assumption here is you have products and services that target customers are willing to pay for; a sales funnel; and you can sell.

Question 7:
Is your business worth doing?

This question is all about money and viability. You need to be totally sure that your idea is worth doing. If you are going to invest your time and money into this business you want a result, right?

If I asked you to invest $10,000 into my business what would you want back? You'd want *at least* $10,000 back - to be cash neutral - but I think you'd be disappointed with that break-even result. I'm sure you would want *more* than $10,000 back. Otherwise why bother?

VCs want a multiple on their investment of at least 3-5 times. Or they want equity share. Or both! For example, *Dragons* want equity expressed as a percentage, such as 30%. They want equity because if the business sells they will get 30% of the final trade sale price.

I once ran a business where if we bought a piece of equipment we were looking for a ten-fold return on that purchase. We bought a commercial printer for $7,000 and came up with a business plan for making $70,000 in additional sales revenues.

When I hired a sales guy on $50,000 a year salary his *'business plan'* was to make at least $500k in sales. I'm not saying your plan should be ten times. It might be four or six times. It can be whatever you feel is normal for your industry.

A plumber says his apprentices cost him $15 an hour but he hires them out at $75 an hour. He needs to get at least a four-fold return to cover his costs of having that staff member.

Matt is an accountant who bills out his team at 3.5 times their hourly rate. That charge-out rate covers non-productive or non-billable activity. His *productivity* rate is about 53% so he needs to cover the 47% of non-productive or unbilled time!

But I meet people who borrow $25,000 and struggle to make the repayments. There is not a ten-fold or four-fold or two-fold plan in place.

Warren spent $75,000 on a piece of equipment. I would have planned for that equipment to generate at least four times the purchase price, per annum.

The workshop teaches you to explore at least nine other related elements. A quick stress test of Warren's plan revealed other oversights. As did Alex's original idea.

This is the value of cross checking.

So the questions are:

- Is your business worth doing? And how do you know?
- What is your revenue target for this year, next year,
- and year three?
- What are your projected costs?
- What is your margin?
- What is your profit target?

Look at revenues and costs – especially costs (including the cost of finance) and margins. Say your plan is to make $1m this year but your costs are $900k. Would you be happy making $100k net profit?

Let's say you find a way to reduce your costs by 5% ($900k x 5% = $45,000). That might increase your profit by 45%. So instead of making $100k you now make $145k.

I meet too many business people who are terrible with business finances.

They don't understand the basics of management accounts (balance sheet, income and cash flow statements). There are no revenue projections (based on size of market, for example).

I met a consultant who left a well-paid job earning $120k a year to start his own business. He still made $120k but lost a huge amount of his earnings on tax, and he worked twice as hard to make the same money plus he was now doing the work that his team previously did.

Plus he missed a subtlety. In the past he was billed at $100 an hour. He was still charging $100 for the hour but taking two hours to do the work so in effect his actual charge out rate was $50 an hour! *Average hourly rate* is the true yardstick.

It got worse. When we calculated his *unpaid* workload his actual hourly rate was less than $16! Starting his own business was really buying himself a low paid job.

I cannot emphasise enough the importance of a good accountant or business planner on this one question.

Whatever happens in your business can be measured and therefore managed better. Therefore how do you measure success in your business? How will you measure success?

The obvious answer is in revenues and costs.

Charles Coonradt has been asking business owners, to create *scoreboards* and *dashboards* that measure activity that impacts revenues and costs. His book *Managing the Obvious* is prescribed reading.

Here's an example of how I have applied Coonradt's approach to measuring.

I was working with Barry, a lumber yard owner and his homework was to identify anything unnecessary that was costing him money or wasting money.

He discovered that they spent a lot on waste removal fees. I asked him to investigate further.

Apparently nine times a week he had a waste removal company come and empty the large metal skips filled with broken timber.

"Broken timber ...? How did it get broken? Does it arrive broken or does it get broken after it arrives?"

Barry went to work to discover the answer. It turned out that when his staff reverse the forklift they reverse into the timber racks. Barry discovered the aisles are too narrow for a forklift to easily perform a three-point turn. Invariably, they reverse into stacked timber.

Over several weeks Barry moved each timber rack. This was quite a logistical feat but it meant a driver could comfortably reverse or turn a forklift. Within a month they had dropped from nine skip pick-ups a week down to one a week.

Steve runs a supermarket and he knows they throw away 60% of the fresh deli items that have a fast perishable shelf life. We were able to reduce that down to 18% through clever in-store marketing.

In both of those examples, knowing the numbers meant better solutions that dramatically reduced waste and costs.

Of course I measure revenues but I have implemented dashboards for the business that give timely, accurate and meaningful feedback that depicts activity and trends that enable my clients to be more proactive.

Your turn

How do you know your business is worth doing? Business plans focus heavily on your financial projections.

The assumption test

The big assumption here is the business will wash its face. Your projections about sales revenues, costs, margins, profits need to be conservative and realistic.

Another assumption is you've really done your due diligence.

But before we go to *Question 8*, let's take a quick look at how you accountant looks at your business.

Three success factors
that your accountant is looking for

While on the topic of money, since 2008, I've run a regular workshop called *How Money Flows Through Your Business.*

Business people who attend this workshop typically say they finally understand what their accountant has been telling them for years. In some cases they even claim they understand their business much better than their accountant!

An accountant basically looks for three things in any business: *growth, profit* and *liquidity.*

Growth is measured in the *Balance Sheet*, which essentially tells us the *value* of your business at any fixed point in time, such as *As At 31 May.*

It shows assets and liabilities but includes cash-at-bank, equity, debts and borrowing, fixed capital and working capital (tax, receivables, payables and inventory).

Profit is measured in the *Profit and Loss Statement* or *Income Statement,* which essentially tells you the *vitality* of your business over a given time, such as, *For the Period of May 1-May 31.*

Basically the *Income Statement* reports on Revenues, Cost of Goods Sold (or Cost of Doing Business), Gross Profit (GP), Overheads, Tax and Costs of Finance and Net Profit (NP) position.

Liquidity is measured in the *Cash Flow Statement,* which essentially measures the *viability* of your business over a given period of time. The *Cash Flow Statement* draws on information from the *Balance Sheet (*adjustments from the *Working Capital* and *Fixed Capital)* to determine the *Operating Cash Flow* and *Net Cash Flow* position.

Combined, these three statements make up what are called *management accounts.* You would generate a set of management accounts periodically - monthly, quarterly or as needed. But essentially your accountant is looking for *growth, profit* and *liquidity.*

But so is an investor.

If you go on *Dragons' Den* or *Shark Tank* they will expect you to be able to explain the performance of your business using these key metrics: the *Income Statement* (P&L), *Revenues, COGs, Gross Profit, Overheads* and *Net Profit;* and relate that to the business valuation.

So it helps to understand these metrics.

If you want a plain language introduction to management accounts download my book *How Money Flows Through Your Business* on *Kindle* available on *Amazon.*

Two Key Drivers

The key business drivers of *growth, profit* and *liquidity* are *Revenues* and *Costs*.

*Revenues i*s all about *making* money. *Costs* is all about *saving* or *keeping* money.

Business should be quite simple: *make a lot more money than you spend.* If you make $1 but spend $1.39 to make that $1 you are in trouble.

But business is more complex than that. You can be making good sales and still have no cash!

A struggling small business approached me for help. They were earning revenues of $14k a month but had no money for bills and wages and couldn't understand why.

I asked if they had taxes to pay, bills to pay, late paying customers or excessive money tied up in stock. I asked about their overheads and costs of finance. In short, the money was on the books - it just wasn't in the form of cash, (liquid).

My client couldn't understand where the money went. After some basic financial education my client located the *missing* money in the *Balance Sheet and Income* statement.

They made sales, but their costs of doing business and overheads were high. Plus they owed money to suppliers, had tax bills and had money tied up in stock.

A young couple took redundancy and poured all their life savings *and* a business loan into a fresh food business. They sold fresh crème to a selection of health food deli's.

The business quickly gobbled up their $75,000 redundancy package and they had to keep topping up their business loan to keep the business afloat.

I asked about *Cost of Goods Sold*.

Let's pretend that their fresh crème wholesaled for $1 but their cost to produce was 77 cents per unit. This left them with a gross profit of 23 cents to pay overheads, taxes and make a profit. That's why they were in trouble.

They were actually funding the operating costs of the business through credit cards and top-up loans.

Their accountant had given them the *same* information but the couple did not understand basic business finance: when you sell something *there's a cost to sell something*. It wasn't hard to forecast the demise of that business.

I advised them to revise their costs of goods sold, reduce overheads and increase margins. Focusing on sales was suggested but their costs merely kept pace with revenues.

A company turning over £1m had costs of £900k. Their net profit was £100k. They engaged a business coach who took their turnover to £1.2m but their costs went to £1.1m. Net profit was still £100k but they were working harder for the same money.

It doesn't matter how much money you make. If your costs are too high or run closely parallel to your revenues you are running a *zombie* business that fails to grow in value and exists to repay the loan. Banks hate *zombie* businesses and so do investors.

And so should you.

Four places where all your business problems live

All businesses have problems. To imagine you will have a problem-free business is totally naive. In fact, the more successful you get the more problems you will generate, but you will get better at handling those problems. There are loads of things that can go wrong in your business but after many years I whittled them down to just four key problem zones in any business that I always focus on as a business coach.

One part *makes* you money (revenues) and the other three *costs* or loses you money (costs).

The activities that *make* you money are *marketing and sales.* If you have problems in marketing and sales, you will have *Revenue* problems that will impact growth, profit and liquidity.

The activities that *cost* you money are *management and administration* (and include HR in this category); *operations* (and include IT and logistics); and *financial control.* If you have problems in these three areas you are losing money.

167

If you have problems in management and administration, operations and financial control – or all three – you have a *Cost* problem and that definitely will impact growth, profit and liquidity. If you have problems in both the Revenues *and* Costs areas then your business is headed for trouble.

When I work with a business that is under-performing or struggling that's where I start looking. But ultimately I see everything as either a *Revenues* or a *Costs* issue that will invariably impact growth, profit and liquidity. To make it simple here's a helpful diagram:

Growth	Profit	Liquidity
Balance Sheet	Income	Cash Flow
Value	*Vitality*	*Viability*

Revenues	Costs
Marketing	Management and
Sales	administration
	Operation
	Financial Control

In summary, a proactive accountant will be able to tell you if:

- your business is growing
- your business is profitable
- your business has good liquidity and cash flow
- you are making money (Revenues)
- you are wasting or losing money (Costs)
- and where exactly the problems are showing up most in your business.

This vital information should result in a detailed action plan and be subjected to close monitoring and a periodic progress review by a qualified accountant.

Question 8
What is your business model?

Let's think about the right business model for your business. Are you a retail shop on the High Street? Are a wholesaler? Or is yours an online, e-commerce site? Is yours a boutique offering or a scalable entity? You're looking for the best business model.

For example, *Amazon* has pretty much forced the High Street bookstore out of business. I am sorry to admit, I buy on *Amazon*. *Amazon* is an e-commerce site that enabled them to reduce the costs of books globally.

High Street video stores holding physical DVDs are long gone. *Blockbuster* was replaced by video streaming and *Netflix*.

When I was a kid I used to go to my local record store. They've all but disappeared.

Spotify and *Apple Music* have changed the way we consume music. And the music charts!

Sheldon could have opened a gallery but he's taking artwork sales online. Sheldon's business model is called an *switchboard* model not unlike the old-fashioned telephone operator that connected one party to another. Sheldon sits in the middle. Like *eBay* and *Amazon* his website will connect sellers and buyers. He will earn a listing fee and a commission fee for selling. Even *Sotheby's* is a switchboard model.

Amazon is also a high volume/low margin business. *Wal-Mart* is a high volume/low margin business but the business model is based on retail outlets and a buying hub. No surprise that *Wal-Mart* are currently going head-to-head with *Amazon*.

Amazon's business model is called a *J Curve* business that requires *Amazon* to keep tipping money into this business before it becomes profitable. Believe it or not *Amazon* is reportedly not yet trading profitably.

With a *J Curve* business expect a lot of financial downside before you see any financial upside. Sheldon's business is a *J Curve* business so he might be in for a shock. What seems like a very simple business idea, may very well run at a loss for some time.

Business models are all about control.

Jean Paul Getty made money drilling for oil but made a lot more money shipping oil. He acquired usage rights to rolling stock and railway time – neither of which he owned - and made a fortune freighting other people's oil on rolling stock and railway lines he didn't own either.

A client sells electricity contracts. He doesn't own the national grid or the infrastructure but he has acquired lot of large, influential customers and controls a wonderful buy/sell wholesale rate with large energy suppliers.

A lot of business start-ups are based on low margin/high volume business models especially e-commerce businesses.

I once spoke to a coach who was trading time for money. His business was a retail one-to-one consulting model. He wanted to take his IP online through e-courses and workshops and failed to realise that in deciding to do that he would essentially become an events business.

What have you decided is the best way to get your products and services from your hands and into the hands of your customers that is efficient and cost effective?

FedEx used to have planes criss-cross the USA, which was very expensive. Now they fly short return trips to central hubs, unload and reload, and fly back to base, a model now adopted by most postal services.

Business models are ultimately about control and cost.

This requires a lot of discussion and careful thought to explore your options.

Right now there is a lot of vacant retail space in Main Street and High Street and some very attractive lease deals - short term. But you might lease a cheap retail store only to find your customers shop online.

Helen sells hair care products. As a hairdresser she realised there were huge margins in hair care products. She could have opened a High Street salon but instead she carefully reviewed online beauty sales, sourced her products from *Alibaba* and created a *Fulfilled By Amazon* business. She now sells hair care products online via *Facebook* to the USA from her bedroom in southwest London!

It is possible if you do your homework and due diligence.

- What's the best delivery system for your business?
- What do you need to control?

Your turn
What is your business model? Why that one? What insights did you get from this section?

The assumption test
The big assumption here is you've picked the right business model that not only consistently delivers a quality result but also delivers the financial results.

STARTING!

Question 9
Are your systems and processes documented?

If you don't have documented systems and processes I can predict you will lose money through inefficiencies.

Sam Carpenter runs a successful call centre in Oregon, USA. But it wasn't always that way. In his best-selling book, *Work the System* he describes the early days of the business as pure chaos. He worked seven days a week, which impacted his marriage and health.

Then he had an epiphany. Drawing on his experience as a electrician he realised that the national grid is actually a series of interconnected systems. And 98.9% of the time those systems work perfectly!

When you go home tonight you expect to flip a switch and lights come on, right? Turning on a light in your home requires the following system:

Light switch > house wiring > fuse box > meter box >
power line > junction box > sub station
> national grid > power station

As an electrician Sam studied the specifications manuals that described each and every system so he could quickly problem-solve power disruptions. Oregon experiences sub-zero winters so people want power failures resolved quickly.

When Sam looked at his own call centre business he realised next to nothing was written down or documented.

"Even our most benign systems were haphazard. We had 25 ways of answering the phone depending on how hung-over you were from the night before! It was totally ad-hoc."

"There is an optimal way to do anything if you invest some time in finding it. Now we have one way of answering a phone no matter who you are or what kind of day or night you've had. We train staff to answer that way and monitor their calls and best of all – it works."

I meet client after client who say if their business works, it's a happy accident. They *have* routines but nothing is written down. There are no documented systems or processes.

But there are too many downsides to winging it every day.

- **It wastes a lot of time.** Basically you are relying on training and memory to make things happen.
- **It's expensive.** A client confessed he recently spent four hours trying to process an online payment for $35 because his regular bookkeeper was away on holiday. At his hourly rate that was an expensive transaction.
- **It's dangerous.** Sometimes you have checklists to ensure that people stay safe. An electrician had to disconnect a sub-station cable running 25000 volts … from memory!

So Sam said, "We had nothing written down. It took us at least three months to get the basics documented but very quickly we started to see the benefits."

One of my clients runs a waste management company. Over a six-week period he started to document the basic health and safety practices. Just having in-truck checklists has resulted in less accidents and safer and more accurate pick-ups.

Dent, the entrepreneur training company took 18 months to document their systems and that has enabled the company to be rolled out internationally in six countries.

Those systems have become IP and have given the company a higher investment valuation.

The results are three-fold.

- Everything runs more smoothly.
- Documentation has enabled the owners to scale that business.
- The valuation of that business has increased. This means if the business is ever put up, as a trade sale the book value is higher than a company without documentation.

Documentation is the primary reason why business brokers can charge substantially more for a franchise.

Importantly, documented systems and processes enable owners to scale the business.

Ray Kroc knew the McDonald Brothers had a successful fast food business but couldn't franchise it. They had tried and failed. Kroc documented their systems and the rest is history. He devised systems a 14-year-old could follow.

I have been working with an accountant for over a year to document their basic systems. It takes time but the productivity gains have more than covered their investment in time and money.

So the questions are:

- Are your systems and processes documented?
- Is this a boutique business or is your intention to scale your business?
- Therefore is your business model scalable?
- Can it be replicated (the cookie cutter concept)?

And:

- Is it valuation or exit-ready?
- Do you want to sell your business?

You may not want to sell your business right now. But when you are ready proven documented systems will make a huge difference to the exit valuation and therefore the price your business can command from a merger or a trade sale.

I have also worked at the other end of the exciting start-up stage of a business – guiding owners when it comes time to exit.

Business owners either exit with a valuation, or with nothing. Worse they exit with debts and insolvent. You should aim to exit with a valuation. Even if you don't want to sell your business right now you should run your business as if it was ready to sell.

Is your business salable right now?

I advise you to run it as if it was! Let's pretend you want to sell your business in the future. The time to think about being exit-ready is now, right from the get-go.

Just think if you were buying a business from someone else. What would you want to know? What documentation would you want to see? Run your business as if one day you might sell it, even if you don't want to sell right now.

Your turn

This is a big section. What insights and actions came from this section? Do you need documented systems and processes? If so, what systems and processes do you think you need?

The assumption test

The big assumption here is thinking you can run a great business without systems!

Question 10
Is it working? How will you know?

This is really a review question.

For starters, you should review the key insights you have taken from this workshop? What did you learn? What were the takeaways? And the action steps? Did you end up with a *to-do* list? Or a *not to-do* list? Is your business idea clearer?

Importantly, did you identify any flawed assumptions? Or opportunities?

You may have even discovered interesting answers to your questions that surprised you. But for now reflect on what you gained from this activity.

I'm also hoping that you started to see relationships between the elements. For example can you see the obvious link between customers, marketing and sales? Or team, delivery and systems?

If you watch a show like *Dragons' Den* they constantly link these elements. What is your idea? What will you sell? How much? To whom? How will you market to them? What is the cost to manufacture and sell price? Retail or wholesale? Can it be taken online? Can it be scaled? Can you reach that audience? How many have you sold so far? And so on.

Longer-term, reflect on how you will know your business is working. Usually you will be hitting key targets and milestones.

For example, a goal for the *Threshold* group is to push through the £83,000 revenues VAT threshold.

But you might have goals that relate to work/life balance. You did not start a business to work longer hours and see less of your family. You started your business to have better family time. Will your business generate that result? How will you know?

Remember, you were looking for assumptions.

Ultimately, how do you feel now you have completed the workshop? Do you need to do the workshop again? A lot of people do!

The assumption test

The big assumption here is you care enough about the success of your business to do this activity properly.

Part 6
What's next?

STARTING!

I've answered all the questions, now what?

When I complete a business strategy with a client and we've answered all the questions, I focus on *insights, cross-checks, action steps* and *review items*.

Insights

I have never yet worked with a client that did not get meaningful insights about their business from this process.

Sometimes they get confirmation that the business idea is OK to proceed, just as it is.

Sometimes, the client pivots. Alex decided to switch from selling mobile phone handsets to sourcing grant funding for downloadable mobile phone content. Dr Rene, the doctor who treats psoriasis modified her offering and niched down to very busy, time poor executive women suffering from hand, neck and face psoriasis. Her value proposition and pricing model altered significantly and positioned herself as a high-end specialist.

Helen did not open a High Street salon but runs a successful haircare products business from her back bedroom.

Sheldon's blinding flash of the obvious was he should beta test his concept on *eBay* - *first* - before he attempted to start his own e-commerce site. He discovered that *eBay* worked just fine; but has noticed that in the two years he has been selling artwork on *eBay* there are *still* not enough artists to justify a dedicated online art gallery or the expense.

Sometimes clients simply park the idea.

Warren's idea was to survey shipping vessels for hull damage. He soon realised he was under-resourced in cash, expert staff and equipment. The idea is currently on hold.

He does however, subcontract his expertise back to oil and gas companies as an interim and uses their staff and equipment. So, a good compromise. It's good because Warren could have easily pushed on with his idea and lost a lot of money.

So:

- What insights have you taken away from your session, so far?
- What jumped out at you? What were the big takeaways?
- What seems obvious to you, now?
- What problems or obstacles seem obvious?
- What needs to be resolved?
- What changes might you need to make to ensure your idea is even better?
- What opportunities did you become aware of?

Cross-checks

When I worked with David Robson in 2010 on *Success in 80 Days* the cross-checking activity was exhaustive to say the least. We cross-checked every single variable against every other single variable, one at a time. And there were lots of variables!

In this method, cross-checking is nowhere near as onerous but it still generates invaluable insights; and it needs to be done to generate those insights.

For example, if you start with the *Idea* and contrast it with *Target Customer* what are the obvious connections?

Dr Rene's *Idea* was to specialise in the treatment of psoriasis. Her approach takes 16 weeks to improve gut health and another 12 weeks to reintroduce a suit`able diet - nearly

40 weeks. Not everyone has the time or money to undergo the gold standard testing, the three-month intensive weekly visits or the ongoing monthly treatments.

However, when Dr Rene conducted a customer analysis she discovered that the patients that got the best results were executive women. They had the money, they made the time, and they were highly motivated. So, a cross-check resulted in Dr Rene niching down to executive women.

Here's a snapshot of Dr Rene's notes where she crosschecked the *Business Idea* with the other variables.

Here's Sheldon's cross-check of the *Business Idea* against the other variables. You can see he was already starting to get a heads up on the logistical issues such as shipping and insuring artworks in transit. And note: no revenue projections!

```
IDEA  Sell our work online art gallery
ARTISTS — collectors. = ebay ???
```

	Target Artists Painters	Collectors
who pay? Big hassles No systems logistics cost		
Online ecommerce But: Shipping Returns Insurance, ESCROW damaged items who pay	TEAM: Me / IT guy	$25000
$$ Borrow $50 000 Yr1 Y2 Y3 ? ?? ?	MARKET Big awareness campaign Do I have budget?	

```
           SELL
website |  Listing  |  sell, ship  |  ?
ecomm   |           |  insure      |
```

Mocking up a simple grid like the ones above will allow you to see the relationships between each key category more clearly.

Interestingly, when you cross-check *Target Customer* against *Team, Market* and so on I guarantee you will get important distinctions missed on the first round of cross-checking.

Action Steps

I really hope you are seeing the obvious outcome of cross-checking - *action steps* - either a *to-do* or a *not -to-do list!*. I'd be very surprised if you do not identify a list of things that need attention either before or after your start your business.

Bernie offers para-legal services to law firms in preparing wills. His cross-check revealed action steps in every category! And some important unanswered questions that need to be addressed such as checklists and compliance. Again, a simple mock-up form of the categories proved invaluable.

Review

Obviously, if you have performed a thorough cross-check, gained insights and listed action steps you are advised to go back and review the original recordings and notes, again. You will add even better insights to your original first impressions. Here's a suggested review process that works well.

Listen back and take notes

If you followed the workshop structure you now have answers for each of the ten categories. And if you did a quick post session review you now have some first impressions, insights and action steps.

But the next step is to take a break - maybe a day or two.

Then schedule time to go back listen back to those original recordings and make notes. I suggest you proceed slowly and listen to one category recording a day. Recently a busy client did this over a two-week period.

Some people create a folder with divider tabs for each category with blank paper. They make notes and keep them in an orderly manner which makes reviewing very easy.

The key is to get answers to the questions and then to review the recordings and add any further insights.

Then start *cross-checking* again. Look carefully for how one area relates to another.

Importantly, you will start stress-testing the assumptions that underpin your business. Some are obvious; some not so obvious. If you rush this process you might miss something important. So proceed at an easy pace.

It's hard for an entrepreneur, but make haste slowly.

Alex's mobile phone project is a great case in point. By doing this workshop carefully Alex pivoted from mobile phone sales to helping App developers get government grants for downloadable content.

Warren's survey business had several major untested assumptions. When he did the workshop, it became patently obvious he lacked the equipment and qualified staff and therefore the capacity to carry out that work profitably if at all. He decided to park the business.

Was that a good thing? I think it is much better to spend your time cross-checking before you start your business.

Of course, there are some things you just can't anticipate until you're up and trading but in my experience, if you've done this process thoroughly those flaws are usually not as detrimental to your success.

The more time you spend on this review part of the process the better the insights and the better your business plan. Of course, you would then have a qualified professional check your final full business plan.

Issues will start to jump out at you – anomalies, oversights, costs, delivery challenges, etc. Alarm bells might sound or you might hear the heavenly sound of the cash register ringing!

Remember, most failed entrepreneurs opted for no planning, bad planning or the wrong plan. That's why this process is invaluable in ensuring your business has the best chance of succeeding.

But you have to be willing to give the process time.

This process has worked for hundreds and hundreds of clients worldwide. They end up with superior business plans that pass the commercial reality test.

Conservatively, this process can easily add significant value to your top and bottom-line. So allow sufficient time and do this part well.

Really lean in, immerse in and value the process.

Write your Business Plan

By 2009, the global financial crisis had changed bank lending policy worldwide. Banks and investors now say you definitely need a written business plan, a solid business case and skin in the game to get funding.

This workshop is therefore even more essential because most entrepreneurs *still* have no plan, a bad plan or the wrong plan. And a high percentage of business plans submitted with a loan application for bank finance still contain unsupported assumptions that do not pass close scrutiny.

This process convincingly helps the entrepreneur to uncover and stress-test the assumptions in their business case. If you complete the workshop you will get invaluable insights that will help you write a more substantial business plan that makes commercial sense.

I recommend you do the workshop *before* you write your business plan.

Once you've done this workshop I highly recommend you visit *The Princes Trust (UK)* website and download their business planning templates. They are user-friendly, incredibly easy to follow and in plain language.

My hope and expectation is that you end up with a business plan that is meaningful and relevant that becomes a plan you will actually refer to often.

This process will certainly help.

Your business plan will be much better thought out, more realistic and better placed to deliver the intended results.

Still undecided?

I am very much aware that some entrepreneurs feel so confident in their idea that even though they agree with everything written here they are still have not made a clear decision to stress-test the assumptions in their idea.

If that sounds like you then you need to pause for thought and consider the implications of doing nothing.

The advice in this book is designed to help you succeed. Ant time spent reviewing your business idea should be seen as a good investment of time on the front-end that ensures you do not waste time and money later on.

Trust me, once you start your business venture you will find it very hard to back track and make time for planning.

I encourage you to do this process and do it thoroughly.

What if I'm already trading?

If you are already trading then you will find this process a lot easier than someone yet to commence trading. Your next step is to run this process as a review of your existing business.

The questions and categories will make immediate sense. You will be able to generate more meaningful and relevant answers and put your insights into action.

I know of companies that do this as an annual review process. I receive feedback that this process generates significant commercial insights that more than justify the time and effort.

The Business Strategy

The problem I have found with entrepreneurs worldwide is they rush into a business start-up, base their decisions on best-case, untested assumptions, and overlook things that in hindsight are glaringly obvious.

Remember: *'You might have a good idea for a business but is there a good business in your idea?'* Getting it wrong can be expensive, a massive waste of time and money and source of stress and heartache. I want you to succeed, and I know you can.

If you have worked through this book and you still feel stuck then consider a 90-minute online business strategy.

If you think a business strategy session would help please contact us. You will get a confidential strategy session, a recording of the session and PDF copies of the session notes.

How to book a session

Please email us at:

https://andrewpriestley.com/contact/

Appendix: The Questions

1. Why

- Why do you want to start this business?
- How will you know your business is working?
- How else will you know?
- What do you ultimately want for your business?
- How can your business be a vehicle for making a contribution and giving back?

2. Your Business Concept

- Tell me what you do at the moment.
- Tell me about your business.
- What's your background?
- What are you doing currently?
- How did you come up with the idea?
- Why did you/do you want to start this business?
- Why this particular business idea?
- Why do you do what you do?
- Is there proof of concept?

3. Your Value Proposition

Target Market

- Who is this for, exactly?
- Who are your target customers?

- Who is your ideal preferred customer?
- Who is your product best suited to?
- Who would you prefer to work with, most?
- Who can afford you?

Problem
- What problem/s are you trying to solve for your target market?
- What are your target customers specifically trying to get done?
- What three dominant problems are stopping your clients from getting the result they want most?

Promise
- What is the promise your product or service makes?
- What's the result I will get?

Positioning
- Are you a premium product or a premium relationship?
- Are you a budget product or a budge relationship?

4. Your Operating Team
- Who's on your operating team?
- Who do you need on your operating team?
- Have you got an organisational chart?
- Have you got written roles and responsibilities and job descriptions?
- Internally (employees/partners) and externally (suppliers/contractors)?
- What does your business actually need?
- Are you resourced OK or under-resourced?

5. Route to Market

Target Market
- Have you conducted a customer analysis?
- Who is your target market? Why them?
- Demographics?
- Psychographics?

Proof
- What is the proof that a market exists?

Route-to-Market
- Describe your route-to-market?
- Are there any barriers to entry?

Sales Process
- What is your sales process?
- How will you sell to your target market?

Competitors
- Who are your competitors?
- Have you conducted a thorough desk search of competitors?

6. Your Product and Services
- What do you sell?
- What do you offer?
- What are the price points?
- What is the cheapest thing you sell?
- What is the most expensive thing you sell?
- Is there any free stuff? Low costs offers?
- What do I specifically get for my money if I was a customer? What's included? What's an extra?
- Have you got a website, or a sales brochure?

- Do you have any website videos or downloadable products?
- Is the sales collateral target customer specific?
- How will you measure success in sales?

7. Is your business worth doing?

- And how do you know?
- What is your revenue target for this year, next year, Year 3?
- What are your projected costs? Margins? Profits?
- Do you need funding or investment?

8. Business Model and Delivery Infrastructure

- What's your business model?
- What infrastructure is required to get your products and services from your hands and into the hands of your customers efficiently and cost effectively?
- How will that work?
- Is your business boutique or scalable?

9. Your Systems

- Are your systems and processes documented?
- Can it be replicated (the cookie cutter concept)?
- Is it valuation or exit-ready?
- Do you want to sell your business one day?
- Is your business salable right now?

10. How will you know it worked?

- What lifestyle benefits do you want your business to deliver?
- Will your business delivering the intended lifestyle outcomes?
- Will your business give you work/life balance?

References

- Abraham, J. (2000). *Getting Everything You Can Out of Everything You've Got.* St. Martins Press.
- Allen, J. (1995). *Visionary Business: The Entrepreneurs Guide to Success.* New World Library.
- Bligh. J. (1998). *Growing Awareness.* John Bligh Nutting Press
- Carpenter, S. (2012). *Work The System.* Greenleaf Book Group Press.
- Coonradt, C. (1984). *The Game of Work.* The Game of Work Inc.
- Coonradt, C. (1994). *Managing the Obvious.* The Game of Work Inc.
- Friedman, W. A. (2004). *Birth of a Salesman.* Harvard.
- Gawande. A. (2011) *The Checklist Manifesto: How to Get Things Right.* Profile.
- Gerber, M. E. (1986). *The E Myth: Why Most Small Business Don't Work and What to Do About It.* Harper Business.
- Harris, M. (2008). *Find Your Lightbulb.* Wiley/Capstone.
- Heath, C. and Heath, D. (2008). *Made to Stick.* Arrow Books.
- Hopper, K. & Hopper. W. (2009). *The Puritan Gift.* I B Taurus.
- Ingram. K. (2017). *Thrive Don't Just Survive.* Rethink Press.
- Jolles, R. L. (1998). *Customer Centred Selling.* Fireside.
- Keller, G. & Papasan. J. (2013). *The One Thing.* John Murray Publishers.
- Lecinski. J. (2011). *Winning the Zero Moment of Truth.* Google
- Lucas, S. (2016). *It's Never About the Fitness.* Rethink Press.
- Morine, F. J. (1980). *Bigger Profits in the 80s.* Cox and Dawes.
- Page. M. (2017). *Simple Logical Repeatable.* Rethink Press.

- Priestley, A. (2015). *The Money Chimp*. Writing Matters Publishing.
- Priestley, D. (2010). *Become a Key Person of Influence*. Ecademy Press.
- Priestley, D. (2013). *Entrepreneur Revolution*. Capstone.
- Priestley, D. (2015). *Oversubscribed*. Capstone.
- Rackham, N. (1996). *The SPIN Selling Fieldbook*. McGraw Hill.
- Rhodes. C. (2015) *House of Commons Briefing Paper, Business Statistics,* Number 06152.
- Robson. D. (2014). *Is Your Business Investor Ready?* Writing Matter Publishing
- Schiffman, S. (2003). *Telesales*. Adams Media Corporation.
- Slywotzky, A.J. and Morrison, D. J. (1997). T*he Profit Zone*. Allen & Unwin.
- Smith. S and Wheeler. J. (2002). *Managing the Customer Experience*. FT/Prentice Hall.
- Stosny. S. Ph.D. (2003). *The Powerful Self.* BookSurge LLC.
- Stosny. S. Ph.D. (2006). *Love Without Hurt*. Da Capo Press.
- Sugar, A. (2010). *What You See Is What You Get*. MacMillan.
- Taylor, D. D and Archer, J. S. (1994). *Up Against the Wal-Marts: How Your Business Can Prosper in the Shadow of the Retail Giants.* Amacom
- Trout, J & Ries. A (2001). *Positioning*. McGraw Hill.
- Waite. R. (2015). *Online Business Start-Up*. Rethink Press.
- Zafron, S. & Logan, D. (2009). *The Three Laws of Performance*. Jossey Bass.

Websites
- www.andrewpriestley.com
- www.dent.global
- www.princes-trust.org.uk
- www.startupbritain.org/startup-tracker/

About the Author

Andrew Priestley is a business coach, speaker and author and in 2017 was listed in the *Top 100 UK Entrepreneur Mentors.*

He is also the head coach for Dent UK and mentors the Threshold Accelerator that helps entrepreneurs exceed the £83,000 VAT threshold.

He works with established SMEs (£300k-£7.5M+) worldwide to deliver a dramatic uplift in revenues and profits.

He coaches ambitious business owners to develop their leadership skills, create a high performing business and to ultimately achieve lifestyle outcomes bigger and sooner.

Andrew says: "You run your business. If your business is running you, you are doing it wrong."

One result of coaching is business owners start thinking and acting more strategically. The typical outcome is a dramatic uplift in performance.

Three common issues seem to be:

- **Leadership** - you might have brilliant technical skills but no formal management training but your business has grown and now demands leadership.
- **Staff issues** - you want a productive high performing team.
- **Strategic/operational conflicts** - your business needs a focus on strategic direction and business performance but you are struggling to let go of the day to day.

To solve these problems he offers:

- A proven approach to developing effective leadership skills that feels natural, intuitive and real
- Structure and high accountability
- Clear feedback and support

Ultimately you start a business because you want it to deliver lifestyle outcomes. Andrew turned his business failure into business success and now teaches others to do the same through one-to-one coaching, workshops, courses, online programmes and public speaking.

Contact Andrew at:

www.andrewpriestley.com

Your testimonials and feedback

Too many businesses fail within the first 12-24 months and this little book has already helped many start-ups succeed. That's why we really appreciate your testimonials and feedback to use in future updates of this book.

Please go to:

https://andrewpriestley.com/contact/

We would especially appreciate your comments and feedback on *Amazon* as well. Thank you in advance for your generous support.

And of course, good luck!

STARTING!

Contact

Email   www.andrewpriestley.com/contact/

Web   www.andrewpriestley.com
                www.dent.global

LinkedIn   www.linkedin.com/in/andrew-priestley-tce/

Twitter   @ARPriestley

Facebook   www.facebook.com/TCE.HQ

STARTING!